Inspirational! Motivat.
Educational! Just some of the words that come to mind when reading Todd Zive's *The Mensch Method*. A must read!

Andrew Terry, Founder and CEO, Terry Associates

*The Mensch Method* offers a refreshing perspective on leadership, emphasizing humility, ethics, and leading by example—a novel approach I've never seen explained this way. I'm excited for the impact it will have on those seeking personal and professional growth across the globe!

Derek Herrera, Founder and CEO, Bright Uro

Todd Zive's *The Mensch Method* is a powerful reminder that success is measured by the legacy we leave and the lives we touch. Truly a transformative read for us all. Ethical behavior and meaningful connections are key to truly embracing the world we live in today!

Kathy Dawson, CEO and President, Dawson & Dawson

Todd Zive's *The Mensch Method* provides a powerful reminder that integrity and empathy are the cornerstones of genuine success, and that true achievement lies in the positive impact we have on others.

Aron Rofer, CEO, Bradley Rofer Foundation and General Counsel, Champions Funding

*The Mensch Method* is an essential resource for transforming adversity into personal and professional growth, an imperative in our turbulent White Water World. With engaging real-life stories and proven practical insights, Zive guides readers to overcome challenges and lead with character.

Leonard Lane, Professor of Strategy, UC Irvine and Corporate Board Member

*The Mensch Method* is a powerful guide to authentic leadership. Todd explores the true meaning of resilience, emphasizing grace, character, and doing what's right. A must-read for aspiring and established leaders alike.

Mickey Gubman, Certified Business Coach and
Managing Director (Retired), Tennant Company

*The Mensch Method* offers simple, yet practical leadership principles that have the power to change lives and make the world a better place for everyone. Todd Zive inspires and uplifts us through his own life story that began in tragedy but is modeled in integrity, generosity, and respect. This insightful and practical guide to becoming a mensch is a model for success every leader should strive for.

Lisa Thomas, Founder and CEO,
Main Street Marketing Partners

Through examples of resilience, determination, and achievement, *The Mensch Method* illustrates how we can lead with integrity, kindness, and purpose—even in challenging times. It proves that success and goodness can and should coexist, showing that it's possible to lead with heart and find fulfillment in both business and life.

John Merlino, Fractional COO and
Former Division President, Lennar

# The Mensch Method

Achieving Success
Through Character
in Life and Business

**Todd Zive**

The Mensch Method: Achieving Success Through Character in Life and Business by Todd Zive

Library of Congress Number: 2024922118

Ebook: 978-1-959009-19-1
Paperback: 978-1-959009-20-7
Hardcover: 978-1-959009-21-4

Published by Simply Good Press Montclair, NJ

# CONTENTS

*To Mindy, Alex, and Marina*
*who inspire me every day*

# AUTHOR'S NOTE

This book draws on stories and examples from my personal experience. I've made every effort to ensure accuracy and authenticity, basing these accounts on my memory, documents, and research. Some stories, events, conversations, and names have also been changed or adjusted to protect privacy.

# INTRODUCTION

Life has a strange way of challenging us, pushing us to our limits, and presenting us with unexpected hurdles. For me, the journey towards leadership and personal growth began with a heart-wrenching tragedy. At the age of four, I experienced the devastating loss of my father when an armed robber murdered him in his pharmacy. This event, though traumatic, set the stage for a remarkable transformation in my life. My father, who I deeply admired, was my first role model and exemplified what it meant to be a mensch. He embodied qualities such as integrity, generosity, and respect for others—core principles that form the foundation of the mensch method which I discuss in this book. A mensch, in its essence, is a person of integrity and honor, someone who strives to do what is right and just, even when no one is watching. The example my father set became a foundational example for my life.

While growing up, I often heard people say, "Be a mensch!" This wasn't just advice; it was a compliment and a call to action. A mensch is more than just a good person—it's someone who lives a life of meaning and impact, both personally and professionally. In business, where success is often measured by profits and outcomes, being a mensch sets you apart as a leader who values people, relationships, and growth.

The word "mensch" comes from Yiddish, a language that was spoken widely in the European Jewish community where my great-grandparents lived before immigrating to the United States in the early 1900s. It's interesting how many Yiddish words—like schmooze, bagel, and schlep—have become part of the everyday English language, often without people realizing where they came from.

Leo Rosten, in *The New Joys of Yiddish*, describes a mensch as "someone of consequence; someone to admire and emulate; someone of noble character."[1] That's a good start, but Rabbi Joshua Hammerman expands on this, pointing out that a mensch embodies at least fifty character traits such as optimism, curiosity, forgiveness, kindness, creativity, gratitude, discipline, enthusiasm, principle, perspective, love of learning, humor, bravery, teamwork, civility, social conscience, and perseverance.[2] These traits aren't just nice-to-haves; they're essential for making a real, positive difference in the world.

Today, more than ever, these values are needed. As Rabbi Hammerman explains, "In a world as dehumanizing as ours has become, simply being a mensch, a kind, honest and loving person of integrity, has become a measure of heroism—and at a time when norms of civility are being routinely quashed, it may be the only measure that matters." We live in a world where people are often focused on their own success and sometimes lose sight of how they treat others along the way. In business leadership especially, there's often immense pressure to focus on financial success, competitiveness, and outcomes. But when leaders prioritize character in the face of these pressures, they build a stronger foundation that benefits everyone—and, in turn, drives long-term success.

For me, the decision to live by these principles became clear as I grew up in the shadow of my father's tragic death. I was faced with a choice: to be defined by grief and despair or to forge a path of resilience and hope. I chose the latter. Embracing the challenges life threw my way, I found strength in adversity and learned that the true measure of a person is not how they fall, but how they rise. With unwavering determination, I pursued my dreams and aspirations, vowing to build a meaningful life and honor the memory of my father. This journey was not one I walked alone; it was significantly shaped by the support of others who provided guidance, encouragement, and companionship at critical moments.

Surrounding myself with positive influences was crucial. I discovered how to lean on others and how to allow them to lean on me. As a young adult, appreciating the importance of hard work and holding myself to my standards helped me become the person I aspired to be. This foundational belief guided me throughout my career as I encountered various challenges and opportunities for growth.

One of the most poignant moments of reflection in my journey came years later during visits with a key father figure and mentor in my life, who was also a highly successful businessman. As he faced his last days before losing a battle to cancer in a quiet hospital room, the presence of his usual formidable demeanor gave way to deep, introspective conversations. I listened intently as he shared his final thoughts. He spoke not of the material success or personal achievements he had known, but of the relationships and people he had encountered along his seventy-five-year journey. In those final days, what mattered to him was the impact he made on others and whether he had done the right things during his life. I shared with him the significant impact he had on me, my wife, and our two children, expressing our love and understanding of his decision to cease cancer treatments.

His words resonated deeply with me as he expressed a sense of peace and fulfillment from having lived a life focused on others and enjoying the experiences of visiting different places around the world. He talked about the simple acts of kindness, the mentorship he provided to professionals, the lives his company helped save, and the love and time he devoted to his family and community. These, he said, were his true achievements. Such a profound exchange made me deeply reflect on my own path—had I truly focused on what matters most? This experience reinforced my belief in the importance of leading a life defined not by what we acquire, but by the positive influence we have on others. It underscored a crucial lesson: the essence of true leadership is found in the legacy we leave behind; in the lives we touch and improve.

Just as there are countless definitions of leadership, so, too, are there countless definitions of success. Since success is subjective and different for everyone, how will you know whether or not you are "successful" then? I've found that a more helpful measure is whether you are fulfilled. This understanding of success helped shape my approach to both personal and professional endeavors, ensuring that my goals align with my values and bring genuine satisfaction.

As I shared my story with others, they responded that they felt inspired to do something similar in their own lives. They appreciated how I had shaped my personal journey and were curious how I had gone about it. This reinforced my belief in sharing knowledge and experiences to empower others on their paths.

Life's unpredictability has taught me that we never truly know what each day may bring. This doesn't mean living every day as if it's your last, but rather being open and aware of the endless possibilities each day holds. From the early tragedy in my family to numerous unexpected events throughout my life—both positive and challenging—I've learned the importance of embracing the unknown with openness and readiness. Such events remind us of the fragility of life and the value of living according to our deepest values.

As my career advanced, these lessons took on new meaning. I reached a high level of corporate leadership, building successful businesses and thriving teams by embodying the principles of servant leadership. This approach of lifting others up and rising together, integral to the mensch method, contrasts sharply with those who ascend alone or diminish others along their path. I found myself continuing to question traditional notions of leadership that equated authority with power and status rather than with influence and character. This reflection led to a realization: leadership is not about wielding power but about empowering others. It is about setting an example through your behavior and decisions, inspiring others to rise above their circumstances and achieve their full potential. Throughout this journey, the willingness to receive support and the courage to seek help when needed are instrumental in overcoming challenges and achieving goals.

Inside my book, you'll find a mix of stories from my life and others, along with practical lessons and insights. The chapters explore core principles such as resilience, building confidence, nurturing relationships, and taking responsibility for your actions.

They guide you through personal and professional growth, covering themes like knowing your strengths, putting in the necessary effort, trusting the process, and caring for yourself and others. You'll also learn how to navigate challenges, stay focused on your goals, collaborate to achieve success, and go after what you want with confidence. Each section offers both inspiration and practical steps to apply these concepts in your own life, with exercises at the end of each chapter to help you on your path to leadership and fulfillment.

I believe there is a different path to success—one that never requires you to sacrifice character or integrity. This path, which I call the mensch method, is about leading with honor, fostering resilience, and living a life of impact. Being a mensch—someone of integrity and noble character—is about more than achieving success; it's about how you achieve it. It's about the legacy you leave and the lives you touch.

You will discover through the pages of this book that leadership is inherently within all of us. It can be cultivated and developed through intentional actions and choices, regardless of where you are in your career or life. Whether you are just stepping into your professional journey, seeking to pivot mid-way, or striving to leave a lasting impact at the pinnacle of your career, you are already a leader, capable of great influence and impact.

Join me on this transformative journey. Let us embark together on a path that embraces challenges, leverages our unique experiences, and uncovers the leader within each of us. As we proceed, you will find a blueprint for leadership that is rooted in authenticity, driven by values, and aimed at creating a positive, enduring impact—one step at a time.

By embracing your personal journey and the principles laid out in this book, you can become the leader you aspire to be—a leader who motivates, empowers, and leaves the world better than you found it. Prepare to be inspired, to challenge your perceptions, and to take action. This book is your guide to being a mensch in leadership and in life. The journey starts now. I believe in you. Let's begin.

## CHAPTER ONE

# A MENSCH CHOOSES RESILIENCE

> When life throws you a curve, you can become angry,
> depressed, or defensive—or you can put your energy
> into learning from the situation and developing
> creative ways to comprehend and respond to it.
>
> Larry E. Senn, *The Mood Elevator*

I was a happy, slightly mischievous kid growing up in the late 1970s in a small town just outside of Springfield, Massachusetts. As the middle of three boys, I took it upon myself to act as a peacekeeper and troublemaker, which may be why my mother's journals from that time refer to me as both "Prince Charming" and "a devil." She also wrote that I had a passion for fixing things, even if they were not broken. This was undoubtedly something I picked up due to my admiration of my father, who had a similar knack for household repairs.

My father, Leslie, was a pharmacist who owned a drug store in the little town of Easthampton, about twenty-five minutes from where we lived. To me, he was Superman, in part because he dressed up as him for Halloween in 1979 when I was four, but mostly because of who he was as a person. Dad was the first mensch I ever knew.

Each day when he came home from work, I ran full speed to greet him. As he walked through the door wearing his white short-sleeved lab coat and a smile, I threw my arms out and gave him a big kiss. I always giggled when he gave me one back.

I wanted to be just like Dad. When I wore my own Superman cape for Halloween that same year, I thought I was making strides. My fondest memories with him are of the days he took me to his pharmacy. I'd entertain myself by doing grown-up things like sneaking around to the pharmacist's side of the prescriptions counter and childish things like playing peekaboo throughout the store.

The best part of the pharmacy was the soda fountain, which was common in drug stores at the time. Lined with round red vinyl stools, the soda fountain's counter ran the length of the store. Behind it were all the ingredients needed to serve up soda and ice cream and—my personal favorite—milkshakes. The most popular drink was called a "dishwater," which was carbonated water mixed with a few squirts of chocolate syrup. The menu also offered egg, tuna, and grilled cheese sandwiches, as well as hot dogs and hamburgers with a side of chips.

Thanks to the soda fountain, Dad's pharmacy was not only a place where people went to pick up their medications but also a gathering spot where locals regularly came to have a treat and socialize. They ordered coffee and toast in the mornings and flooded the counter at lunchtime, requiring Dad to hire two additional employees to serve customers during the lunch rush.

On Sunday mornings, however, the store was pretty quiet. At the time, it was a local law that businesses had to be closed on Sundays. But since people needed prescriptions filled every day of the week, pharmacies were an exception. So, Dad ran the drug store on Sundays, too. Since there was a lot of downtime and it was a short workday, these were usually the days my older brother, Brian, or I would go with him. Our younger brother, Keith, was still too young, so he usually stayed home.

Dad taught me all kinds of lessons on those Sunday mornings: greeting customers and being kind, cleaning up after myself when my chocolate milkshake dripped down the sides of the tall glass and onto the counter, counting change, and straightening the displays. These were my earliest lessons on being a mensch, centered on how to respect people and take care of the world around me.

Dad brought me to work so frequently on Sundays that it was a miracle I wasn't there on Sunday, June 8, 1980. It's hard to call it a miracle, though, considering the events of that day brought about the greatest tragedy of my life.

## How Adversity Found Me

On that Sunday, my father went to work at the pharmacy per his usual routine. For some reason, Brian, Keith, and I stayed home. Later that day, two police officers knocked on the front door of our house and changed our lives forever. They told my mother that my father had been found in the pharmacy's cellar with a gunshot wound to the head. A cabinet containing narcotic drugs was found open and empty. Dad was thirty-five years old, and his now fatherless boys were seven, four, and two.

At the time, I did not understand what the police officer was telling my mom about my father's violent death. I only knew that my mother was crying hysterically, and I eventually realized that my hero was never coming home.

A comprehensive investigation began, spanning five states and involving multiple agencies. Investigators were able to link the bullet's shell casing to a .22-caliber black semi-automatic Ruger pistol and eventually arrested a twenty-eight-year-old man. The seven-week trial to convict him of first-degree premeditated murder was one of the longest trials in Hampshire County's history.

The prosecuting district attorneys were David Ross and Bill St. James, both of whom are mensches and continue to keep in touch with my family. Thanks to their exceptional work and the support of many others, the murderer was convicted on May 30, 1981, and sentenced to life in prison.[3]

While justice had been served, the conviction didn't bring closure for my family. On multiple occasions, he petitioned to commute his sentence—the first instance being just four years after my father's murder. Each time the murderer submitted such a petition, we were asked to support the district attorney by providing documentation and statements about the hardships we endured because of the murderer's senseless act so that his sentence would not be commuted. The response to his requests for release didn't come for months, and as we waited, we couldn't help but wonder: if he were to be released, would he hurt other people? Would he come after our family, seeking revenge for his conviction? Dredging up painful details of our past and present, then waiting anxiously to learn whether Dad's murderer was going to walk free, was a retraumatizing experience every time we went through it.

Fortunately, the murderer's attempts to gain his freedom continued unsuccessfully until he died in prison in 2015, more than thirty-five years after that tragic Sunday morning. His death brought an additional level of closure, but it still did not end the pain. For thirty-five years, this man woke up every morning—12,971 mornings that my father could have had with his wife and sons, but of which we had all been robbed. While we eventually learned to live with the pain, we would continue to feel the weight of this tragedy throughout our lives.

## The Aftermath of Adversity

Each member of my family reacted differently to the loss of my father. For me, the confusion was overwhelming. I bombarded my mom with questions: Where is Daddy? Can I see him? Can he see us? Why can't we dig up the box he was put in? Does he get cold in there? Does dirt get in the box? Where is the robber? Who is going to throw the baseball with me now? Though Mom always answered honestly and kindly, I know these questions only added to her pain.

My mother, Eydie, did her best with the terrible hand she was dealt. She did what she believed was right, but understandably, she carried a lot of anger. In the aftermath of my father's death, not only did she have to bear her immense grief, but she also had to fill the roles of two parents and figure out how to support three young boys. She suddenly became the financial provider, the cook, the repair person, the kid shuttler, and the manager of my father's pharmacy business—all while the district attorneys prepared and conducted her husband's murder trial, a process which lasted almost a year.

It was far more than anyone should be asked to handle, yet Mom stepped up to the challenge and took her new responsibilities incredibly seriously. Eventually, she had to close the pharmacy in 1981, but she provided for us, cared for us, and filled our hurting home with as much love as she could.

Mom also had a temper, something I experienced more vividly in the years following Dad's death. This was probably due in part to my own lashing out, which I did frequently during those days. I attribute the rest to her being stretched too thin, which naturally lowered her patience and tolerance. Regardless of the reason, I completely understand why she referred to me as both Prince Charming and a devil because she regularly faced off with both versions of me.

Lashing out seemed to be my way of dealing with the questions that continued to circle in my young mind, especially the ones too heartbreaking to voice aloud. I had lost my hero and couldn't reconcile how that was possible. Superman was the strongest man in the world and faster than a speeding bullet. So how had my dad, my Superman, been killed by one? If I had been there, wearing my cape, would my four-year-old self have been able to protect him somehow? Would I still have a father to greet at the end of each day or someone to throw me on their shoulders to see over the crowd at a baseball game? I eventually accepted that there was nothing I could have done to prevent this tragedy. Despite all my questions and regrets, all I could do—all any of us could do—was try to find a way to move forward. But finding a path to resilience was no easy feat.

At ten years old—six years after my father's death—I was still embroiled in an emotional battle. My suffering became so intense that it showed up as physical symptoms: painful headaches, dizziness, lethargy, and vomiting. After extensive testing, doctors ruled out any physical cause for my symptoms, so my mother sought the help of a psychologist. In her journal entry on May 16, 1986, Mom wrote a letter to me, which I recently read for the first time.

"Sometimes it takes a while to deal with reality," she wrote, explaining that I understood more now at the age of ten than I had at the age of four, and that as I got older, I would continue to process what had happened. Still, she added, there were certain things about Dad's death we would never understand. Drawing on her mensch mindset, Mom's guidance was clear: "We cannot question what happened; we can only say, 'Now that this has happened, what are we going to do about it?'" And this is precisely what she did. Mom modeled resilience for us boys in how she lived her life and led our family.

## Finding a Way Forward

Around the age of eleven, my path to resilience began to take shape. I was finally old and strong enough to carry a shovel filled with snow, so I started going outside to clear driveways after each snowstorm. Considering we lived in New England, this was quite often throughout the winter. After clearing my own driveway, I went door-to-door in our neighborhood, earning about ten dollars for each driveway I shoveled. Some weekends, I spent the entire day shoveling snow. During the weekdays, the street plows often created new piles of snow that blocked driveway entrances, giving me even more opportunities to shovel when I came home from school.

As a young boy still processing the devastating death of my father, this work gave me a much-needed sense of independence and purpose. It also got me out of the house and into the peacefulness of nature. After a snowstorm, hardly anyone was outside, and the streets were silent. The air was clean and fresh, and sometimes as I shoveled, the snow still fell quietly from the sky. When I was outside, I focused on working hard and helping people, which was the best feeling of all. My neighbors appreciated my work and always told me what a good job I did. I felt a deep satisfaction when I saw the difference I could make, turning an inaccessible driveway into a clean and clear one that the homeowner could easily pull into and walk on without slipping.

Soon, I was making a good amount of money (for a kid) and enjoying my newfound sense of independence. I used my earnings to invest in a lawn mower, which I brought around to the same winter customers in the spring and summer. Mowing brought back happy memories of sitting with my father on his ride-on mower and cutting our lawn together.

My business continued to expand as I began washing windows throughout the neighborhood. I bought a leaf blower to help clean up leaves that fell from the trees in the fall (always taking care of my own home first). I was determined to succeed, and that determination helped me find a way through my pain. I learned about perseverance, making commitments, and helping others. I developed self-worth and self-reliance. Unbeknownst to me, by developing this small business as an entrepreneur, I also created an important foundation for my professional future and found my path to resilience.

## Resilience Inspires Others

As I got older, my business of mowing lawns and shoveling snow expanded into helping others in different ways. In high school, I began volunteering at Shriner's Children's Hospital in Springfield, Massachusetts. Initially, my goal was simply to fulfill my volunteer requirement for the Key Club Service organization to which I belonged. But I ended up embracing the experience, gaining a humbling lesson in resilience along the way.

At Shriner's, I visited children who had it really rough, suffering from severe orthopedic ailments and other medical complications. One patient in particular, Anna, was about eleven years old when I first met her. She was from Puerto Rico and was at the hospital because she had a significant curvature of her spine. As part of her treatment, Anna wore a halo-shaped brace around her head. Because of the pins inserted into her head from the halo, she was at high risk of infection. Before visiting Anna in her room, I had to put on a special yellow gown to help ensure her safety. Yet every time I visited, Anna had a smile from ear to ear. Like her, all the kids at Shriner's had plenty of reasons to gripe about the unfairness of life, but I never heard them complain.

Shortly after I began volunteering at the hospital, my weekly two hours of volunteering became fifteen hours, then twenty or more, spanning weekends and weeknights whenever I could squeeze in a visit. When the children told me how much my visits meant to them, I was grateful to know that something so simple on my part could brighten someone else's life. I enjoyed being of service to them and realized they were also of service to me. Taking care of others felt as if I was also tending to my own pain. These children turned my sadness into gratitude and gifted me with a new outlook. If they could persevere and find reasons to smile, so could I. Eventually, the impact of my resilient attitude expanded beyond my service at the hospital.

I continued to discover more ways in which my attitude could impact others, including through team sports—baseball in particular. My dad was a sports fan, and I have faint but cherished memories of watching games with him. Over time, participating in sports became a way for me to feel connected to him and bond with other father figures like my coaches. Being an overweight kid who was often bullied, I found that sports also helped me gain confidence and improve my self-esteem. As I became more skilled as an athlete, I improved my fitness and made friends with my teammates.

During my junior year in high school, I was the starting catcher on the varsity baseball team. Being a catcher was a tough, high-pressure position, but I loved being in on every play. I often came home from practices and games with new bruises on my forearm or bicep area from all the balls I had blocked with my body. Mom usually found me with my arms wrapped in bandages, holding big ice packs in place. During that season, I spent countless extra hours doing baseball drills in the evenings and on weekends. Sometimes the pitchers wanted to practice and needed someone to catch for them. Of course, I was always willing to volunteer.

In the spring, after finishing a successful season, we were all looking forward to celebrating at our team banquet. When I arrived, I was surprised and excited to discover that, in addition to the players' families, school staff, and team supporters, a local news station was also there.

After dinner, our coach presented several awards, saving the "Jeff Vinick Never Give Up, Never Give In" award for last. Jeff had been a three-star athlete at our high school and tragically died of cancer shortly before turning nineteen. The local news station was there to cover this award and bring awareness to Jeff's story.

When I was announced as the recipient of the Jeff Vinick award, I was extremely honored. As I approached my coach to receive the award, he described to the audience the work ethic I had shown throughout the season, highlighting my willingness to always help out my teammates and consistently put in extra effort.

Receiving that award was a turning point that solidified my path to resilience. Since my father's murder, I had committed myself to finding ways to move forward. I never gave up and never gave in. I hadn't thought that anyone noticed my work ethic, considered the adversity I had to overcome, or recognized that I taught myself how to play baseball without my father there to practice with and coach me. Of course, I hadn't put in all that effort for accolades or recognition by others. But the acknowledgment from my coach and teammates showed me that my resilience and determination could inspire others. It made me realize that through my efforts and attitude, I could motivate others to persevere through their own challenges, work harder, and support their teammates. My journey demonstrated that overcoming adversity and maintaining a positive, dedicated mindset could make a significant impact on those around me.

As a young person, I also received other awards and recognition for my effort and attitude. But while awards and recognition are always nice, they are not the reason why a mensch chooses to do the right thing. I learned at an early age that it is important to do the right thing simply to be a good person, not for any recognition.

## We All Face Adversity

Fortunately, you don't need to experience devastating trauma to build resilience. Common hardships—such as failing a test, losing a game, encountering setbacks in achieving your goals, facing financial difficulties, getting let go from a job, or not receiving a promotion—are experiences we all may face at some point in our lives. These moments can leave you feeling gutted and unsure about how to proceed.

However, it's precisely these challenges that provide opportunities for growth and resilience. Failing a test can teach you to reassess your study methods and develop better strategies for learning. Losing a game can show you the importance of teamwork, perseverance, and sportsmanship. Setbacks in achieving your goals can force you to reevaluate your plans, adapt to new circumstances, and find creative solutions. Facing financial difficulties can help you learn to manage your resources more effectively and prioritize what truly matters. Being let go from a job can be a catalyst for discovering new career paths, improving your skills, and building a stronger professional network. Not receiving a promotion can motivate you to work harder, seek feedback, and continuously improve yourself.

A common response in these scenarios is to try to recover from the adversity as if it never happened, to "get back" to where you were before the experience. But that approach usually ends up being a losing battle. If you try to push through like nothing's changed, you'll likely miss the chance to build real resilience. Why? Because adversity changes you in deep, fundamental ways. The things you go through shape you, challenge the way you see the world, and force you to shift your perspective. You can't just go back to who you were before the hardship—doing that would mean ignoring the lessons learned, the emotional scars you carry, and the potential for growth that comes from those experiences.

Even the idea of "bouncing back" can be misleading. It makes it sound like you're supposed to go back to how things were before, but the truth is, you're not the same person anymore. Your outlook, your abilities, and even your sense of what's possible have evolved. Real resilience isn't about going back to some earlier version of yourself—it's about moving forward, using what you've learned along the way to carve out a new path. You don't bounce back to who you were; you grow into who you can become.

On Jim Rome's podcast *The Reinvention Project*, Paralympic medalist and motivational speaker Amy Purdy defined resilience this way: "True resilience has nothing to do with bouncing back to where we once were...it's about accepting what is and bouncing forward to all that we could be."[4] Amy is absolutely right. Although we often use the expression when describing recovery from adversity, you can't go back to what once was.

After my father's murder, the task before me was to accept my new reality and bounce forward. Especially as a child, that acceptance took me a long time to reach, while I also simultaneously searched for a way to move forward. It wasn't about trying to get back to the life I had before, because that life didn't exist anymore. Losing my father changed everything and pushed me to find strength in ways I never expected. But as I developed my mensch mindset, I eventually found my way forward. I didn't bounce back —I grew into a new version of myself, someone who could take the lessons from that loss and let them shape the values that guide me today.

## Importance of Expressing Feelings for Resilience

Growing up, I rarely spoke about what I was going through. The topic of my father's murder was very painful, and I wasn't eager to bring it up. Additionally, almost everyone in my world—teachers, coaches, friends, community members—already knew about the tragedy and what my family had endured. I felt there was no need to discuss it or delve into its impact on me. Drawing additional attention to the situation seemed like it would only draw pity, and that was the last thing I wanted.

At the time, social norms around mental health were different. People didn't talk as openly and honestly about mental health as we do now. It was quite unusual that my mother took me to see a psychologist back then. While my family and friends never discouraged me from sharing my emotions and experiences, they also didn't actively encourage it. Looking back, I realize that expressing my feelings more might have helped me find my path to resilience sooner.

Fortunately, we now have a much better understanding of mental health. We know that expressing our feelings can drive us to become stronger and help us build the resilience we need. As I'll share in later chapters, being open, honest, and vulnerable with others lays a valuable foundation for meaningful connections, which can also help you heal from adversity.

If you are facing adversity and seeking a path to resilience, I encourage you to open up about your experience. Find a trusted friend, family member, or a mental health professional who can support you. We all face challenges at some point or another, so you are not alone. By sharing your struggles with others, you are much more likely to find resilience and the confidence to bounce forward.

In October 1995, I was at the season-opening hockey game of the Boston University Terriers. Two minutes into the game, Terrier coach Jack Parker gave freshman player Travis Roy the go-ahead to get on the ice for his very first collegiate shift. After playing for just eleven seconds, Roy crashed headfirst into the wall and was immediately paralyzed, making him a lifelong quadriplegic. I will never forget the eerie silence that filled the crowded arena as Roy was carried out on a stretcher.

Until his death in 2020, Travis Roy was a powerful spokesperson for overcoming adversity and led a foundation dedicated to helping others with spinal cord injuries. He said, "Sometimes, we choose our challenges . . . but there are other times in life when the challenges simply choose us, and it's what we do in the face of the challenges that defines who we are."[5] In the face of our greatest challenges, adversities, and heartaches, a mensch chooses resilience.

I often wonder, if I had never lost my father, would I still be the same person I am today? I like to think I would still be a good person—that those mensch-like qualities my dad taught me about respecting others and the world around me would have paved the way for kindness and service to others. However, I'm not sure I would have come to understand resilience quite as well as I do. I would have inevitably experienced other challenges, but would I have found as much joy and healing in helping others? Would I have found the same sense of purpose and fulfillment in shoveling snow for my neighbors, which, in turn, formed a foundation for my professional success?

The tragedy of my father's murder laid the foundation for who I have become. I will be forever devastated by the experience of losing him, but I have successfully found my way through the adversity, learned from it, and am a better person because of it. Throughout my childhood and into adulthood, life threw plenty of challenges my way, and I faced them with the same resilience and determination that I did facing my father's death. I forged ahead, pursuing my dreams and aspirations, and despite the pain and grief that will forever linger, I focused on building a meaningful life.

We all face different types of adversity. For you, it might be a certain fear, an ongoing struggle, or a pervasive feeling of loneliness. Or perhaps it's the end of a relationship or an unexpected career change. Regardless of your challenge, we are all responsible for figuring out a way to move forward and take control of our lives. As the movie character Rocky Balboa famously said, "You, me, or nobody is gonna hit as hard as life. But it ain't about how hard you hit. It's about how hard you can get hit and keep moving forward."

# Exercises

1) Reflect on Past Adversity.

   Think of a time in your life when you faced adversity. How did you respond? Reflecting on that experience, how might you respond differently to similar challenges in the future?

2) Identify Admirable Characteristics.

   Think of someone you know who has overcome hardship in their life. Write down three characteristics you admire most about this person.

   a)

   b)

   c)

3) Learn from Resilient Individuals.

Have a conversation with this person and ask how they developed those characteristics.

Based on this person's input, identify one to three actions you can take to strengthen your own resilience.

a)

b)

c)

# CHAPTER TWO

# A MENSCH BELIEVES IN THEMSELF

The more you believe in your own ability to succeed,
the more likely it is that you will.

Shawn Achor, *The Happiness Advantage*

We're all familiar with the expression "believe in yourself." It's been used so often that it has generally lost its effectiveness. But to be a true mensch—to achieve your personal ambitions and to be a successful leader—you *must* believe in yourself. But what does this actually mean?

Believing in yourself is more than simply having a positive attitude and overcoming self-doubt. At its core, self-belief is about trusting yourself: trusting who you are as a person, trusting in your own competence and abilities, and trusting those you've chosen to support you. Self-belief is about standing up to the naysayers and the negative influences you will inevitably encounter along your journey and remaining steadfast in your convictions through it all. To make the right decisions at the intersections along your path, you need to learn how to listen to your own voice and have confidence in yourself.

## The Power of Self-Belief

In 2010, I was responsible for the largest product line at a leading medical device company, reporting to the Vice President of Global Marketing, Glenn. Over the following years, Glenn exemplified the characteristics of a mensch in both his personal and professional life. He always tried to do the right thing and continues to be a great person who works through challenges with resilience, drawing strength from his faith and the support of others. He empowered and challenged me to become the best I could possibly be. After working on his team for four years, he began his transition into retirement from the medical device industry, and I was promoted to fill his position.

This change meant that colleagues who had previously been peers or seniors to me were now going to be under my leadership. Although I had positive working relationships with all of them, some may have developed a bias against me due to my younger age and rapid trajectory to my new position. Many might have wondered whether I could succeed in the new role as the department leader.

But I didn't wonder. I had been preparing for that role for years, and although I had a touch of imposter syndrome, I held fast to my self-belief. I reminded myself of my competence and experience. Above all, I was confident that my mensch mindset would see me through. I knew that if I believed in myself and continued to do the right thing, I could succeed just as Glenn had.

Sure enough, my department performed extremely well. We met our goals year after year, grew from ten to seventy members, expanded our capabilities into new functional areas, and helped the company consistently achieve its revenue and profit targets. I also developed a strong reputation for empowering, developing, and coaching high-performing leaders at all levels across the company. In a local business journal's "Best Places to Work" survey, my department received the highest overall rating for all departments at our company of over three thousand associates. My own self-belief had evolved into a team belief that led to our collective success.

In his book, *The Happiness Advantage,* Shawn Achor writes, "The more you believe in your own ability to succeed, the more likely it is that you will."[6] The power of our own mindset is huge. Visualizing success, building self-assurance, and doing the work are essential to manifesting your goals. The simple act of telling yourself you are capable and that you will succeed often leads to positive outcomes.

## Follow Your Intuition

For as long as I can remember, I have always had a desire to fix things. As a child, I loved taking apart our telephone, television, and radio, then putting them back together. I also had an affinity for math and science, which were by far my strongest subjects in school.

I was a teenager in the fall of 1989 when a 6.9 magnitude earthquake struck the San Francisco Bay Area. As a die-hard baseball fan, I had been watching the live TV broadcast of the World Series championship game held at Candlestick Park when the earthquake suddenly shook the stadium. The quake led to a ten day postponement of the game as authorities assessed the widespread damage across the region. I couldn't stop watching the news coverage and was intrigued by how an earthquake could drastically impact so many buildings and the area's infrastructure.

Among the damage was the collapse of the top deck of the San Francisco–Oakland Bay Bridge. The "fixer" in me was preoccupied by the fact that the damage to the bridge could have been prevented if engineers had properly designed it to withstand an earthquake of that intensity.[7]

Three years later, as a senior in high school, I was applying to colleges and choosing a major. Driven by my passion for fixing things, my interest in math and science, and the lessons I learned from the earthquake, I decided to pursue a degree in civil engineering. I wanted to gain the knowledge and skills to plan, design, and oversee the construction of buildings, roads, and bridges, ultimately helping to make the world a safer place.

In the fall of 1993, I left my home in Massachusetts and traveled halfway across the country to study at Washington University in St. Louis, Missouri. As I entered college, I expected to love the experience. I had seen the excitement of my older brother, who couldn't wait to return to his college after being home with us during his holiday break. However, this was not my experience. Soon after starting my studies, I felt like something was missing. Although I was doing well in my courses, I struggled to find enjoyment outside of the classroom and missed being near home. To bridge this gap, I explored various activities such as joining friends on excursions in the city, camping in the Ozark mountains, exploring different fraternities, and spending time in the public park near campus. While some of these offered enjoyable moments, I could not shake the feeling that my overall college experience was lacking.

I reached out to my father's cousin, David, who had been a mentor of mine throughout my childhood. That spring, he took me on tours of the major universities around Boston. When I visited Boston University, I was impressed with its cutting-edge biomedical engineering program—an engineering discipline that combines mathematics, engineering, and biology to improve healthcare. At the time, it was also one of the very few universities with an accredited program in this branch of engineering. The more I learned about this new field, the more excited I became. I envisioned myself improving the lives of individuals similar to the children I had met during my volunteer experiences at Shriner's Hospital.

Making the decision to transfer from my civil engineering program at Washington University to the biomedical engineering program at Boston University may not seem like a big leap. After all, plenty of undergraduate students choose to transfer schools. At the time, however, it was the biggest decision I had ever faced. I spoke about it with many of my peers, who mostly responded with questions like, "Why would you want to leave Washington University?" One person even said outright, "You're crazy. That's a terrible decision."

As you make decisions along your life journey, you will inevitably receive input and opinions from others, whether solicited or not. Some people will give you valuable, thoughtful input while others might make snap judgments without knowing enough about your situation.

In these moments, it is crucial to ensure your voice is included in the orchestra of input, along with the voices of those who have your best interests at heart. When it came time to make my college decision, Mom and other family members gave the best input. All they wanted was for me to pursue my passion. Mom asked, "What is going to make you happy? What do you want to do?" David emphasized that the steering wheel of my future was in my hands, and it was up to me to take a turn if I wanted to. I just had to step on the gas and take a chance.

Despite the support of my closest family, I still had doubts and uncertainties. I faced a decision where the best choice was not entirely clear. Should I take a chance on something unknown or stay in a familiar but unhappy situation? Following my gut, I decided to take a chance and transferred to Boston University.

Changing my major and colleges was one of many challenging decisions in my life. It led to graduating with a degree in biomedical engineering and my first job as an engineer. This experience taught me that your original goal can change, and your path can take unexpected turns, but it doesn't mean that you've done something wrong. Such transitions are a natural part of life. The key is to trust your intuition and follow the path that feels right for you.

After working for about four years as a biomedical engineer, I took another big risk: I changed careers. Though I was successful as an engineer, I believed that I could make a bigger impact and be more fulfilled on a different career track. I had a natural mind for business and a personality that was well-suited to working closely with people. In my engineering role, I spent most of my time on a computer designing devices and had limited interaction with others outside my product development team. I wanted to engage more with customers in hospitals and help them treat their patients more effectively.

I also noticed that in the medical device industry, there were individuals who were highly skilled at sales and marketing but unfamiliar with the technical intricacies of the products. Similarly, many engineers lacked the ability to effectively connect with customers and fully understand their needs. I saw an opportunity to leverage my unique skill set to improve the connection between customers, sales representatives, and engineers. A role in product management at an innovative medical technology company seemed like the perfect fit. However, making such a change was not straightforward. I had limited experience in sales and marketing, and while engineers were in high demand, marketers were not.

As I considered making this switch, there were plenty of critics: "You trained as an engineer; you should be doing engineering," and "Why would you want to be a salesperson or marketer when you can be an engineer?" I listened to their opinions but allowed the most influential voice to be my own, and it was telling me to take the leap. So, in 2002, I made the switch from engineering to product management.

During my first role as a product manager, my supervisor highlighted that my unique background and perspective would enable me to collaborate closely with the engineers. Having taken many of the same courses, I "understood their language." Rather than holding me back, my non-marketing background became an asset that set me apart from others. From that point forward, I never worked in a dedicated engineering position again, but continued a very successful path in business while working closely with engineers.

Taking a risk does not always result in immediate success. However, without taking those chances and making those changes, I would not have achieved the significant personal growth that I did. *Success is not a straight line.* It zigs and zags, starts and stops, and undergoes various transformations along the way. The most important thing is to continually assess the intersections you encounter and, when you have a decision to make, trust in your ability to choose what is best for you.

## Don't Listen to the Naysayers

Listening to your intuition is hard when the voices of naysayers try to drown it out. From changing colleges and majors to pivoting from engineering into business, I encountered my fair share of them. Even after settling into my new career, those voices never went away entirely. Many people overlooked me and didn't believe I was capable because my path was different from the conventional one. However, I had full confidence in my potential and chosen path. To proceed successfully, I had to block out the doubts of others around me.

A few years into my new career, I was invited to attend a meeting with Walter, my manager, and Jack, his manager, along with several others from different departments. The meeting was for Walter to present to Jack the status of an ongoing product launch that Walter was leading.

During the meeting, things quickly became heated as Jack was clearly unhappy with Walter's update. Jack began scolding Walter in front of the whole group. Aside from the sounds of Jack's outburst, the room was silent. A few of the others looked on anxiously, hoping not to become the next focus of Jack's frustration.

Walter tried to respond diplomatically, but he had barely gotten a word out when Jack snapped, "You know what, Walter? When you're knocked down on the mat, instead of trying to get up, sometimes it's better to just stay down." I'll never forget hearing this demotivating comment. It stirred all kinds of feelings and questions in my mind. Is this the attitude of the company I'm working for? Is this their idea of "leadership?" I had made it my life mission to never "stay down on the mat" when I faced adversity, yet here was someone communicating just that to one of their team members.

In that moment, I realized that my consistent choice to get up and keep going was more than mere resilience. Somewhere along the way, I had realized an essential truth: the most important voice to listen to is your own. When you have faith in yourself and are willing to take risks, regardless of others' opinions, an experience of being knocked down can transform into a learning opportunity for growth.

## Stay True to Yourself

Inspiration can come from many places, and the metaphor of the carrot, egg, and coffee bean is a profound illustration of staying true to oneself. Imagine a challenging environment represented by a pot of boiling water. Consider the first item, a carrot. When a carrot is initially placed in the pot, it is hard but eventually becomes soft and mushy. Next, there is an egg. The egg's inside starts out as a vulnerable liquid but is protected by a hard shell. However, even with this hard shell, the egg's inside also becomes hard in the water. The last item is a coffee bean. What is remarkable about the coffee bean is that even in a pot of boiling water, it remains largely unchanged. Yet it transforms the boiling water into coffee.

The carrot and the egg represent people who allow themselves to be influenced by a negative environment. The carrot becomes mushy, like someone who feels beaten whenever they face adversity. The egg is like a person who tries to use a protective exterior but still lets their environment change who they are on the inside. People who work in an unhealthy environment can ultimately succumb to it. The coffee bean, however, is like a person who remains true to themselves, no matter how bad the environment is around them.

When I first heard this metaphor during an interview with Damon West on Jim Rome's podcast *The Reinvention Project*, the message immediately resonated with me. If you are in a tough situation, surrounded by a negative culture, you can be impacted or changed by your surroundings, or you can choose to believe in who you are and forge ahead.

This is the choice I made when faced with naysayers both early in my career and throughout the years that followed. Though I was not always able to change my environment, I ensured that the pot of boiling water never changed me. Instead of being the carrot or the egg, each challenging situation became an opportunity for me to be a coffee bean.

## Speak Your Truth

When I was a director of marketing at a medical technology company, the executive leadership team was a year into the process of finding a replacement for an executive who was transitioning into retirement. The requirements for the job were extremely specific, and competition among the candidates was very high. Our emphasis on cultural fit was one of the main reasons we hadn't yet found the right person for the role. After a long search, everyone was excited about a strong candidate who was being considered. I was asked to be one of the interviewers.

The day after my interview with the candidate, I entered the executive conference room for the debriefing session. Seated at the middle of the long oval table was the hiring manager. I was almost directly opposite him, and we were joined by six other colleagues who had also interviewed the candidate. Our recruitment director initiated the discussion, asking for feedback.

First, she asked the interviewer to her left. He gave a pretty neutral answer, not too positive or negative. The next leader did the same, and it seemed like nobody wanted to come across as too opinionated, especially with all the time and challenges involved in filling the position.

Then, it was my turn. Nerves overwhelmed me as I began to share my thoughts. Addressing the hiring manager directly, I said that I felt the candidate was not a suitable fit for the role or our company and explained my reasoning. His expression remained unchanged, but my anxiety shifted from expressing my viewpoint to wondering how it was being received.

As the next interviewer spoke and agreed with my feedback, a wave of relief came over me. Yet I still wondered about the hiring manager's thoughts. He finally confirmed that the candidate was indeed not the right fit and then turned to the recruitment director, instructing, "Please ensure that Todd is involved in the next candidate's interview." With those words, I silently let out a sigh of relief.

In this case, I was asked for my opinion and, despite the pressure felt from the ongoing search for a replacement, I knew that being honest was most important. While I was initially afraid of disappointing the hiring manager, I knew that withholding my true thoughts would neither be helpful nor appreciated, even if my openness meant our search would have to continue. A few weeks later, we interviewed another candidate who proved to be a good fit. I shared my feedback, and the company ultimately hired her.

Believing in yourself enough to speak your truth shows others your competence and reinforces it within yourself. Self-belief means standing by your perspective and having the confidence to share it. While it is not always easy or immediately appreciated, honesty and authenticity will always serve you best.

As my path has twisted and turned, none of my successes would have occurred had I not taken chances and believed in my ability to meet each new challenge. As authors Alan Stein Jr. and Jon Sternfeld express in *Raise Your Game*, "Self-doubt is the number one success killer and...you can either sit around and wait for an opportunity or you can create one yourself."[8] People often fail despite having the capability, resources, and community they need to succeed because they lack the drive, motivation, and essential belief in themselves.

My self-belief didn't mean that I accomplished everything I set out to do. It didn't prevent me from reaching a point in my career where I felt "stuck" and wasn't sure what to do next. But no matter the outcome, the trust I have in myself has always given me the confidence to pivot when needed and grow into the person that I want to become.

Your path through life will inevitably twist and turn. Who you are in your twenties is not the same as who you are in your forties, fifties, or sixties. Your goals might change along the way, or different ways to reach them might appear unexpectedly. To find the path that is right for you, believe in yourself and listen to your own voice. Prioritize your voice over others', and when you are down on the mat, make yourself get up.

# Exercises

1) Reflect on Resilience.

Describe a time when you were knocked off course. How did you find your way forward? Who or what inspired you to get up off the mat? What dreams, aspirations, and/or motivations gave you the courage to believe in yourself?

2) Identify Positive Characteristics.

Identify three positive characteristics you see in yourself. Return to this list and build on it whenever you need a boost of confidence to get through difficult or unexpected circumstances.

a)

b)

c)

## CHAPTER THREE

# A MENSCH CONSIDERS THEIR INFLUENCES

The people you surround yourself with influence
your behaviors, so choose friends who have healthy
habits.

Dan Buettner

In the summer of 1997, I had just finished my fourth year at
Boston University and was set to graduate after one more semester
in the fall. To celebrate this milestone, I planned a backpacking trip
through Europe with two friends, Don and Tim. My intuition told
me it was going to be an unforgettable experience, and it ended up
being just that, but not for the reasons I expected.

I knew Tim from Washington University and Don from Boston
University, but they had never met. It wasn't until shortly before
boarding our transatlantic flight from New York to London
that they were introduced to each other. Our adventure started
smoothly. We arrived at Heathrow Airport after a redeye flight
and checked into our youth hostel. However, after five enjoyable
days in England, our group dynamics began to deteriorate once
we arrived in Paris.

Don and Tim had different interests and personalities. Tim loved exploring museums, taking photos, and sampling local foods during the day. Don, on the other hand, preferred to go to dance clubs throughout the night and sleep until noon. Striking a balance between the three of us proved to be challenging and caused significant tension, particularly between Tim and Don.

Navigating the fine line between these two friendships was a real test. Despite my desire to remain impartial, I found it hard to ignore my suspicions about Don's behavior. When he did venture out during the day, his actions were questionable. I noticed things like merchandise peeking out from beneath his clothing as we quickly left a shop, or his sneaky entries into various tourist sites without acquiring a ticket. What caught my attention even more was the distinct, adrenaline-fueled smile that would flash across Don's face each time he successfully pulled off one of these stunts. His behavior only added to the issues our group was already facing.

Despite how uncomfortable Tim and I were with Don's behavior, we tried to make the most of our trip and continued to Switzerland and Italy. About a week later, on a Friday morning, we woke up promptly at 9:00 a.m. to catch the 10:30 a.m. train from Rome to Florence. We arrived at the station with just a couple of minutes to spare but learned that the train we planned to take was a special express train, considerably pricier than the local lines that fit our budget. After some confusion and panic, we managed to find a more cost-effective option and, before long, we were on our way.

The train was hot and stuffy in the blistering summer heat. When we tried to lower our windows for some fresh air, they wouldn't open, forcing us to sweat through our clothes. As you can imagine, this uncomfortable situation did little to ease the discontent among our group. Soon, we had enough and decided to get off the train at the next stop, right in the middle of Tuscany.

Since we had skipped breakfast in our rush to catch the train, our first priority was to find a good meal in the small town of Camucia. We stumbled upon a charming restaurant and sat at a small round table on the patio. Lunch was delicious, but conversation was sparse. After finishing our meal, we paid the bill and headed to a nearby hostel. Don got a single room with a view, while Tim and I shared a double across the hall. Once we were settled into our rooms, I decided it was time to clear the air with Don.

I found him standing on his third-floor balcony overlooking the rolling green hills and charming buildings below. "Why don't we invite Tim out here so the three of us can talk?" I suggested. "I bet he'd love to see this; we don't have a balcony in our room."

Don barked, "Tim doesn't deserve to see this. He obviously has a problem with me, so why should I be nice to him?"

Determined not to let Don continue down this negative path, I responded honestly, telling him how his behavior on this trip had upset both Tim and me, and that we wanted a different dynamic moving forward. But Don exploded. "Why are you both being like this? Maybe I should finish this trip without you!"

As I opened my mouth to protest and assure him that we wanted him with us, I found myself unable to get the words out. I asked myself if Don was the kind of person I wanted to share the rest of this journey with. The answer was a resounding no. For the first time, the thought of completely parting ways with a friend entered my mind.

"Maybe that would be for the best," I responded, knowing that Tim would agree. Our intention to resolve things evolved into a discussion about the most amicable way to go our separate ways, which we did the following morning. Since that day, I haven't seen or spoken with Don. Tim and I went on to have a great adventure for the next several weeks through Europe. With Don gone, the tension disappeared, and every day felt lighter, more fun—just the way I imagined the trip would be.

Looking back, I started thinking a lot about friendships and the kind of people I wanted around me. I realized how important it was to have people in my life who genuinely made it better. In that moment, the values that really stood out to me—integrity, respect, and honesty—became even more important. These are the values I strive to live by as a mensch, and they helped me decide which relationships were worth keeping.

At the time, it wasn't an easy decision. Cutting ties with someone I'd shared memories with wasn't something I took lightly, but I realized that Don's behavior didn't align with the values I wanted to live by. It wasn't about holding onto relationships out of convenience; it was about making sure the people I connected with embodied the principles that were most important to me.

That's when I learned that doing what's right sometimes means making tough, uncomfortable decisions. It meant choosing relationships that lifted me up and stepping away from those that didn't. If I had continued the trip with Don, it would've only led to more frustration and accepting behaviors I wasn't okay with. Walking away was an act of self-respect, and it ensured I could stay true to the values that mattered most.

In the end, it wasn't just the trip that made that summer unforgettable—it was the lessons I learned about friendship. The people you spend time with shape who you are, and sometimes, letting go of certain people is what you need to grow. That experience solidified my understanding of what it means to live with character, a quality at the heart of being a mensch.

## Social Influences - *Who Do You Roll With?*

Think about my experience with Don, then consider the people you choose to spend time with. In *The Compound Effect*, Darren Hardy synthesized research from social psychologist Dr. David McClellan of Harvard, stating that the people you spend time with "determine as much as 95 percent of your success or failure in life."[9] In other words, you are who you roll with. While we cannot choose our family, we can choose our friends. A mensch is deliberate about who they allow into their social circle and who they allow to influence their path.

My Europe trip with Don and Tim was a microcosm of this reality. The tension I felt between them—two very different people—represented a choice. Which type of person did I want in my circle? More importantly, which type of person did I want to be like? Eventually, the answer was clear, and I had to part ways with Don to remove his negative influence from my life. Had I remained friends with him, I might have become a different person.

As Jamie Villalovos candidly wrote in *Happy and Strong*, "If your friends cuss a lot, you usually will too. If they drink a lot and like to go to the lake all weekend, you usually will too. If they are super negative and complain about their jobs, politics, and their relatives, you may not realize it, but you are most likely a little negative as well."[10]

Surrounding yourself with people of integrity who consistently strive to improve increases your likelihood of personal growth. If your friends prioritize their physical health, you will be more inclined to engage in activities like hiking and healthy eating. If they are resilient and have strategies to manage their mental health, you will likely pick up some good habits for dealing with stress and staying calm under pressure.

Author Shawn Achor has described this as the "super bounce effect." In his book *Big Potential*, he draws a parallel between the "super bounce" one can experience when jumping on a trampoline with a partner and the effect of having supportive people around you. When timed correctly, a jumping partner can compound the energy of their bounce into yours, elevating both of you higher than if you jumped alone.

Achor writes, "The height of your potential is predicted by the people who surround you. So, the key to creating a super bounce for your potential is to surround yourself with people who will lift you up rather than drag you down."[11] The converse of a super bounce is also true. A jumping partner can also steal the energy of your bounce to heighten their own trajectory while leaving you on the canvas. This is why Achor says that when you are lucky enough to find your super bouncers, you should hold onto them tightly because they are golden. "Whereas negative influencers sap your energy, positive people actually provide energy when you are low, which helps you more effectively solve problems, deal with challenges and work toward your goals."[12]

So, how do you find these uplifting individuals? How do you know if you're rolling with the right people? As you develop your own mensch mindset, you can also learn to recognize it in others. Look for qualities and characteristics you want to see in yourself. Trust your instincts. Just as alarm bells were going off for Tim and me during that trip to Europe with Don, you might have people in your life who evoke a feeling that something just doesn't feel right. If someone is sapping the energy out of your bounce, consider removing them from your life if you can. Instead, find the positive influences who will offer you a super bounce.

Whether they are friends, mentors, colleagues, or family members, the people you associate with greatly influence your life. It's important to spend time with those who support and uplift you. Seeking people who "lift you up" doesn't mean surrounding yourself with only those who praise you. As my son's former baseball coach says, "There's nothing worse than a false cheerleader." Instead, find people who believe in you and challenge you. Offer that same encouragement in return. Together, you will soar higher than you could alone.

## Professional Influences - *With whom do you work?*

The impact of your social influences is pretty intuitive, but it can be harder to acknowledge the impact of professional ones. We do not always realize that these are more often under our control. We sometimes feel stuck or that we are "at the whim" of our bosses or our employer, but this is not always the case. A mensch realizes the importance of being selective about their professional influences, just as much as their social ones.

You have the power to choose your environment and the impact it has on you. Align yourself with a company and people who are positive and supportive. You will be elevated. Just like finding mensches to populate your social circle, you can also find companies that possess mensch-like characteristics.

While choosing the right environment is crucial, employers and hiring managers also play a significant role in shaping that environment. They have the responsibility to ensure that new hires will contribute to the team and align with its values. I learned this the hard way when I hired someone without fully considering how well she would fit with our team's culture.

On paper, she had impressive accomplishments and the technical skills we needed. However, I didn't dig deep enough into whether her approach would align with our team's values. Soon after she started, her autonomous nature caused tension and division on the team.

Over her time with the company, she created a silo, building alliances with certain team members. Instead of being collaborative, she focused on her own interests which weakened the team's cohesion. This experience exemplified that skills and experience, while important, aren't everything. A team member's ability to collaborate, communicate, and align with the team's values can make or break its success.

From that moment on, I paid more attention to candidates' interpersonal skills and their ability to grow and adapt. This lesson has stayed with me and reinforced the importance of being selective about professional influences.

## Mentors in Your Corner

In addition to being selective about the companies or organizations with which you engage and being mindful of the candidates you hire, mentors can also significantly contribute to your development. By aligning ourselves with the right people and organizations, we can create environments where everyone can thrive.

I am fortunate to have had multiple trusted mentors over the years. Rich was one of my managers and, with almost twenty years of career experience beyond my own, he served as an outstanding guide to help me shape the kind of leader I aspired to be. He not only exemplified the importance of standing up for what is right but also emphasized the value of authenticity. Rich frequently provided me with timely, constructive feedback, helping me grow and continuously improve.

My dad's cousin, David, has also significantly contributed to both my personal and professional journey. When I was having a very challenging time with a colleague, he provided great advice and helped me develop an effective strategy to improve the situation. We spent several evenings discussing different approaches I could take, analyzing how each move might play out, and considering the potential reactions from my colleague. With his guidance, I was able to address the underlying issues and find a way to work more collaboratively with him. This experience not only resolved the immediate conflict but also taught me valuable skills that I continue to use.

Similarly, Joel was a close relative and mentor who had an outstanding career as the founder and CEO of a highly successful advanced technical ceramics company. He advised me on pivotal career choices and shared numerous practical tips. For example, early in my career, when he was visiting with my family at the kitchen table, Joel said to me, "Iron your shirt!" just before I was about to run out the door to a business meeting with a very wrinkled one. His advice taught me to pay closer attention to important details, a lesson that has stayed with me throughout my career.

Joel also shared an insightful story about one of his company's vice presidents who asked him to be his mentor. In response, Joel redirected the VP's perspective, urging him to embrace the role of mentor rather than mentee. Joel emphasized that executives should champion mentorship within their teams and foster a culture of growth and guidance. I applied this wisdom when I ascended to the executive level myself.

The positive impact of these three mentors on my life has been invaluable and I know that I would not be the leader I am today without them. Having such positive professional influences is key to becoming the leader you aspire to be.

When I offer this advice, the natural question you might have is, "How do I find a mentor?" The process is simpler than you might think. The key is to look for someone who has—or multiple people who have—a sincere commitment to your growth and a combination of the following characteristics:

- interpersonal compatibility
- willingness to invest time
- trustworthiness

- strong background and experience in your field
- ability to provide honest, constructive feedback
- helpful in identifying areas of improvement
- effective communication style
- and, you guessed it, someone who is a mensch!

When you find such a person, you will be amazed by how much the relationship can "super bounce" your career and your life.

## The Power of Peer Pressure

As teenagers, most of us experienced the immense power of peer pressure. However, it doesn't only apply to teenagers; it affects adults, too. During an evening reception at a conference in Chicago, my attention shifted to the bar where I saw a senior leader from another company. He was slurring his words, making inappropriate jokes, and being rude. But his behavior wasn't a solo act. He was surrounded by people from his company and others, all laughing at his jokes and keeping him as the center of attention.

I knew that these people were, for the most part, playing along. They would not have condoned his behavior or considered it appropriate for someone in his position to act that way. While some may have been acting out of fear of retaliation, my sense is that the majority of them had a fear of missing out—of not being included in the interaction. They were concerned that if they did not participate, if they did not feed into the banter from a high-profile leader, then they might not be able to move forward in their career. Someone else would be the recipient of his favor and future opportunities.

This is the grown-up version of peer pressure—going along with the behavior of those around you out of fear of not being accepted or rewarded by those in power.

If I had seen any of my team members engaging with him that night, I would have approached them in hopes of drawing them away from his negative influence. We can't control the actions of others, but we can control our own. So, we should choose to demonstrate positive behavior, hoping that others will follow our example. While peer pressure is often seen as a negative influence, it can also be a powerful force for good.

## Personal Influences - *What Do You Consume?*

The people in your life have a great influence on you. So, too, do the things you consume. You've probably heard the expression, "You are what you eat." If you regularly eat healthy food, you will likely be in better physical health. It's easy to forget that the same is true for what you feed your mind.

If you constantly consume negative media, your thoughts will likely align with that negativity. Similarly, if you constantly compare yourself to others on social media, your confidence will likely decline. Surrounding yourself with pessimism darkens your thoughts, impacting your emotional well-being and often leading to stress, depression, and anxiety. The good news is that you aren't bound to this path. You have the power to create positive thoughts by exposing yourself to uplifting influences.

In recent years, I've become highly intentional about what media I consume in my spare time. I focus on uplifting and inspiring content. In the car, I enjoy listening to podcasts such as *The Ed Mylett Show*, *The Burn Podcast by Ben Newman*, and Jim Rome's *The Reinvention Project*. While I don't watch the news every night, I stay informed on important issues by reading the online edition of *The Wall Street Journal* every day. The difference is, I am very selective about the information I consume and the sources I access.

What you consume includes not only your diet and media but also the hobbies you have and the habits you develop. Establishing a workout routine exercises your body and surrounds you with people who value a healthy lifestyle. If you are active in your religious community, you are similarly surrounding yourself with people and perspectives that are positive and uplifting. The groups and activities you participate in have a direct impact on your overall lifestyle and attitude.

Daniel, a friend of mine, has struggled with constant dissatis-faction over his career path in recent years. I wanted to understand what he envisioned as a fulfilling career, so I asked him about it. In response, Daniel mentioned a few individuals he follows on social media, describing how their posts depict their seemingly effortless success. Curious about the path he believed they took, I probed further. "I could never do that. I'm not good enough," Daniel responded. Although he did not directly answer my question, his honesty revealed how social media had influenced his self-perception.

In an interview on *The Ed Mylett Show*, Dr. Robert Waldinger explains this issue that many of us can relate to. "How we use social media matters in terms of our happiness and our well-being. If you use social media actively to connect with people, well-being usually goes up. If you use social media passively, just consuming content, it often goes down. For example, if we scroll through other people's Instagram feeds—you know, we curate our lives for each other on social media. I post my happy pictures. I don't post the pictures where I wake up feeling lost and depressed or hungover. So, when we look at these curated lives, it's really easy to get the impression that 'God everybody else is having this great life, and I'm the only person who doesn't have it figured out.' So that kind of passive consumption of social media lowers well-being, it can make us more depressed, more anxious."[13]

After several more conversations, Daniel opened up to me. He admitted that his lack of confidence was a stumbling block and expressed his desire to work on it. Over the next few months, his demeanor and self-confidence underwent a transformation, leading to a significant new opportunity within his current company.

When I asked Daniel about the catalyst for this change, he attributed it to his decision to reduce his exposure to social media. He stopped concerning himself with the lives of people he did not know—lives that are largely falsified in their portrayal. Once my friend reduced this influence, he also adjusted his self-talk. He replaced self-doubting statements like "I'm not good enough for this" with positive affirmations such as "I have what it takes to succeed." Instead of thinking, "There's no way I'll get this job," he started telling himself, "I'm exactly what they're looking for."

This same effect can happen in every area of your life. If you fill your mind with encouraging thoughts, you will witness a shift in your self-worth and life perspective. If you surround yourself with messages that you are smart and confident, you will begin to believe it and will behave in ways that reinforce this belief. If you want to stop approaching life with a glass-half-empty attitude, you must train your brain to see the positive.

One way I do this is through a daily gratitude practice. Every morning, I write down three things I'm grateful for from the previous day. This simple habit has transformed my mindset, helping me naturally look for the positive aspects of each day.

Motivational speaker Tony Robbins emphasizes that, "Emotions control the quality of our life. Because your mental and emotional state is the single most important ingredient to not only success but fulfillment."[14] Changing your thoughts doesn't happen overnight, but it starts with changing the ideas and influences around you. When my friend was no longer bombarded by a sense of failure or unnecessary guilt, he found his confidence. By choosing stories, media, entertainment, and even foods that enrich you, you can create a positive outlook that leads to success.

Your influences have a major impact on your attitude, worldview, and life path. Positive energy attracts positive energy. It's important to regularly evaluate who you spend time with, who you work with, and what you consume, as life is always changing. By staying mindful of these factors, you ensure that you will remain on a path of growth and positivity.

# Exercises

1) List your influences in each of the following categories.

Social (the people you roll with):
*

*

*


Professional (mentors or company culture):
*

*

*


Personal (what you consume and participate in):
*

*

*


2) Rate the impact of each influence on a scale of 1-5.

1 = Highly Negative
2 = Negative
3 = Neutral
4 = Positive
5 = Highly Positive

3) Provide a brief explanation for each rating. Why did you assign this particular score to each influence?

4) Identify three positive influences that you can introduce into your life to replace any negative ones. Write down your answers and describe how each new influence could positively impact your well-being and growth.

a)

b)

c)

# CHAPTER FOUR

# A MENSCH KNOWS
# WHERE THEY ARE

Knowing yourself is the beginning of all wisdom.

Aristotle

Living in the twenty-first century, you've likely used a smartphone or navigation system to guide you to a desired destination. You understand that those handy turn-by-turn instructions only work because the device knows where you're currently located. It uses GPS technology to calculate the best route from your location to your destination. It's not enough to just tell the system where you want to go; it can't give you directions unless it also knows your starting point.

The journey of life is no different. To get where you want to go, you must know where you are. This means having a clear understanding of your current situation—your habits, your emotional state, and your surroundings. Whether you're thriving or facing challenges, recognizing your current circumstances gives you the clarity to move forward with purpose.

Equally important, to become who you want to be, you must first understand who you currently are. This involves deeper self-reflection: recognizing your core values, your strengths, and your weaknesses. It's about acknowledging your beliefs and the personal patterns that shape your decisions. This self-awareness is key to charting a path toward growth because it helps you make choices aligned with the person you aspire to become.

Both of these insights—knowing where you are and who you are—are foundational to the mensch method. The mensch method emphasizes leading with character, integrity, and decency, all of which are grounded in emotional intelligence and self-awareness. These traits are common among people who experience true fulfillment in life.

Emotional intelligence is the ability to recognize, understand, and manage your emotions, while also considering how they affect others. It's about being aware of what you're feeling, why you're feeling it, and how those feelings influence your decisions and interactions with others. When you're emotionally intelligent, you're better equipped to handle both personal and professional challenges, maintain meaningful relationships, and stay calm under pressure.

Self-awareness, on the other hand, is about looking inward and understanding how your internal state—your emotions, beliefs, and biases—affects your outward behavior. Knowing who you are means being conscious of these factors and how they impact the decisions you make daily. This awareness gives you the power to lead with greater integrity and intention.

Just like a GPS guides you to your destination, emotional intelligence and self-awareness guide you toward becoming the best version of yourself, enabling you to lead by example and have a positive impact on those around you.

## Be Curious About Where You Are

One morning nearly two decades ago, I walked into the office with a smile and no particular expectations for the day. As I greeted a few coworkers on the way to my cubicle, I noticed that the workspace was unusually empty, lacking its typical flurry of morning activity. I didn't think much of it, though, and went about my business.

About an hour later, my coworkers started coming into the open workspace, all abuzz with excitement. Curious about what was going on, I traced the crowd back to the conference room where they were coming from. I asked someone what was going on, and they told me the company had picked a group of employees for a special development program. It was for those identified as top talent with leadership potential.

As I walked back to my desk, I felt like I had been punched in the gut. My heart sank, and a wave of frustration and disbelief washed over me. How could I not have been included? I'd worked hard, done everything asked of me, and believed I was making an impact. Yet, in that moment, it became clear that the leadership team didn't see the same potential in me that I saw in myself. I felt overlooked, unappreciated, and embarrassed.

I could feel the sting of rejection setting in, and my first instinct was to become defensive. My mind began running through justifications for why I should have been selected, listing all the reasons why they were wrong. I thought about storming into my manager's office and demanding an explanation. But as much as I wanted to react, I knew that anger and frustration wouldn't help me move forward. I took a deep breath and forced myself to pause. Instead of lashing out or wallowing in self-pity, I realized that I needed to see the situation for what it truly was.

Why had I not been included? Was there something about my performance or approach that I hadn't been honest with myself about? What were my blind spots? Instead of letting the pain of being passed over define me, I became curious. I had to confront the possibility that maybe I wasn't showing up the way I thought I was. That thought stung, but I knew if I wanted to grow, I needed to be willing to take an honest inventory of myself.

It wasn't easy. Sitting with those difficult emotions and facing the fact that I wasn't where I thought I should be required a level of humility that didn't come naturally, but I was determined to figure out how to move forward. I asked for feedback from my manager and colleagues to better understand where I could improve. Some of the feedback was hard to hear—there were areas where I needed to step up, skills I needed to sharpen, and ways I could be more visible. But hearing these things allowed me to turn what felt like a personal failure into a roadmap for growth.

This experience taught me that setbacks, no matter how painful, can be transformative. By choosing curiosity over defensiveness, I was able to redirect my energy into becoming the leader I wanted to be. It wasn't about proving anyone wrong—it was about becoming better for myself. And in the end, that's what pushed me forward.

## Look for Blind Spots

In 1998, I was working for a medical technology startup of twelve employees in Boston that was developing an innovative camera system that allowed doctors to view inside a patient's abdomen during surgery. A notable feature of the system was its capability to take photos and store them on a floppy disk, a memory storage device. Having a system that could store images in this way was considered cutting-edge at the time and drew interest from many potential customers.

Camaraderie was strong among my coworkers, and our enthusiasm centered on the pending regulatory approval from the Food and Drug Administration (FDA) for our groundbreaking device. When we finally received approval, we had a pizza party and reminisced about our challenging journey to reach that pivotal point.

With FDA approval, we shifted our focus to conducting customer evaluations. Our first one was scheduled at a hospital in Texas, with less than forty-eight hours to prepare. As the team's Research and Development Engineer, I primarily supported the system's design, conducted tests, and delivered presentations to prospective customers. Given my understanding of the system and flexibility with my schedule, I was asked to fly to Texas to conduct the evaluation.

I arrived at the hospital two hours before the procedure, giving myself plenty of time to set up the system and train the staff. Wearing hospital-provided scrubs, I waited in the back of the operating room for the surgery to begin. About thirty minutes into the procedure, the lead surgeon asked me to turn on the camera. It was my big moment, and I knew exactly what to do (or so I thought). I picked up the cable and plugged it into the unit. Immediately, the surgeon began yelling. It took me a few seconds to realize that he was yelling at me. The system seemed to be working, so I could not understand what I had done wrong.

Apparently, I had touched the top of the sterile drape when plugging in the camera, so I'd contaminated the operating field. The patient was fine, but I was a wreck. I felt as if the temperature had been turned up to 150°F. The surgeon ordered me to leave the room.

Thankfully, the drape was replaced, and the surgery went well, so there was no real harm done. I was glad I had remained calm (if a bit sweaty) throughout the uncomfortable moment, but I felt like I had failed. What was I going to tell my boss and the team who were waiting for an update? How could I have let this happen? Was the company going to fire me? Replaying the incident in my mind, I realized that my mistake was due to not knowing enough about the protocols in the operating room—especially the invisible sterile field. Upon entering such a high-stakes situation, I could have been more prepared.

While I vowed to never repeat that specific mistake, I made plenty of others in the years that followed. I always tried my best to anticipate blind spots and prepare myself as well as I could, but sometimes we don't know what our weaknesses are until they become apparent. The question isn't whether we have weaknesses, but how we will react when we discover them.

## Be Open to Feedback

Even though our blind spots are hidden from our own view, they often stand out to others. This isn't because people are actively seeking to find our faults. There are simply some aspects of ourselves that we cannot clearly see. Others have a different perspective, which allows them to provide insights that we might overlook. As Mark Cuban phrases it, "You don't know what you don't know."[15] Fortunately, the people in our lives who know us can reveal these difficult-to-see areas for improvement. If they are kind enough to give us constructive feedback, our job is to listen with an open mind and figure out the best path forward. Of course, this is easier said than done—particularly when the feedback is challenging to hear.

Many years ago, I was talking with my colleague, Mark, who's from New England, during a coffee break at a conference. We were discussing my team's launch plan for a new product when it became clear from his facial expression that he wasn't aligned with the plan. This was puzzling since it had received positive feedback from other company peers. However, they weren't the ones tasked with executing it; Mark and his team were the ones who would directly engage with our customers on the launch.

With hesitation, Mark said, "Todd, you really need to do a better job of listening to me and my team. We have many concerns and would like the opportunity to be heard." My initial reaction was quite defensive, almost on the counterattack. As I replied, he remained composed. When I finally stopped, Mark calmly suggested that I think about his comments and that we'd talk later in the week.

That night in my hotel room, I thought more about his comment that I needed to listen more to him and his team. At the time, I held a leadership position with a large team, and critical feedback like this was rarely directed my way. However, Mark offered honest and direct feedback. He wasn't trying to make me feel bad; he sought to advance his team and our company forward while also contributing to my development as a leader.

When I saw him the following morning, I thanked him for his feedback. I apologized for my initial reaction and admitted that, while his comments were hard to hear, they were right. Finally, I told him that I was committed to doing better and appreciated his help. In true mensch fashion, Mark replied in a supportive way.

The type of feedback he provided to me was "honest" rather than "negative." As performance coach Alan Stein Jr. wrote with Jon Sternfeld in *Raise Your Game*, "The feedback itself is neither positive nor negative. It's neutral. . . It becomes positive or negative only when we choose to attach feelings and emotions to it."[16] Honest feedback is constructive, not sugar-coated, and is delivered with the intent of being helpful rather than critical. Listening affords you the opportunity to decide whether any changes need to be made and provides you with a framework to go about making them.

Mark cared enough to help me identify a blind spot, and I'm grateful that I listened to what he had to say. By responding thoughtfully to his feedback the following morning, I strengthened my relationship with him and his team, deepened my understanding of my team members and cross-functional partners, and became a more effective leader.

## Be Discerning with Feedback

Mark's feedback was spot on, but not all feedback is. When I was excluded from the high-potential employee meeting, I took a moment to consider how I could improve, but I didn't blindly accept someone else's assessment of me. I knew I had high potential, even if those around me did not recognize it. If I had simply accepted their assessment, I might have become complacent, allowing someone else's opinion to overshadow my confidence.

Distinguishing between constructive and detrimental feedback is critical. It involves acknowledging well-intentioned critique while guarding against false portraits that may erode your self-belief.

## Timing and Delivery Matter

Similarly, when giving feedback, don't become overly focused on what needs improvement. Be sure to also emphasize existing strengths and what is working well. I learned this lesson best as a parent. As my kids were growing up, I gave plenty of constructive criticism but was thoughtful about when and how I delivered it. At my son Alex's youth baseball games, rather than shouting advice between pitches while he was at bat, I spoke with him before the game. We talked through some of the skills we had been working on, and I offered a few last-minute reminders. But in general, I found it was most effective to simply boost his confidence. Before he'd take the field, I would remind him, "You've got this. You've been practicing and working hard. You'll do great." Once it was game time, I simply cheered him on.

My experience in the corporate world was similar to how I supported Alex on the baseball field. In business, I learned that people need to be ready for feedback for it to be effective, and that timing is critical. Asking, "Can I give you some constructive feedback?" made people more receptive than if I had surprised them with it. "The compliment sandwich" is also useful, where you deliver constructive feedback between two positive observations about someone's performance.

Regardless of how it's delivered, when you're on the receiving end of feedback, listen carefully to what people have to say and respond with appreciation. You might decide to change course, or you might not. Whatever you decide, you can accept their perspective for what it is and be grateful for the opportunity to consider a potential weakness that you might not have been aware of.

## Blind Spots Can Be Cultural

Blind spots are not only found in workplace practices and procedures; they can also come from cultural and social differences. Our varied upbringings in different cultures can lead to significant differences in how we work, communicate, and relate to others. When we become too used to our own experiences, we start seeing the world through a particular lens and can develop cultural blind spots.

My own cultural blind spots became evident as I transitioned from growing up in a small community in western Massachusetts to living in a diverse college environment and later working in Boston. The workforce in the city was filled with people of all religions and races, exposing me to different cultures, beliefs, and communication styles.

As my career evolved on a global scale, my travels exposed me to different cultures and customs. For example, interactions with French colleagues highlighted the contrast in communication styles—Americans often balance constructive feedback with positive remarks, while the French usually have a more direct approach. The first time I experienced this difference was during a conversation with one of my French colleagues who gave highly critical and direct feedback on my team's commercialization plan. I was initially stunned but quickly realized that this was the communication norm in their culture.

My trips to Asia—specifically Japan, Korea, and China—taught me about cultures deeply rooted in respect, especially in how they welcome out-of-town guests. Unlike the typical American reaction, where hosting can sometimes feel like an inconvenience, my hosts in Asia were always warm and hospitable. They expressed that hosting a guest was an honor.

For example, during a visit to Tokyo, I was impressed by the kindness and generosity of my hosts. They made an effort to communicate in English, and introductions involved bowing and a formal exchange of business cards. I had a similar experience in Shanghai, where my hosts expressed their respect by introducing me to the local cuisine. In Seoul, my Korean colleagues proudly taught me about the history of different neighborhoods as we passed by them while on our way to meetings.

These experiences left a lasting impression on me, not only in how I approach hosting international colleagues but also in my broader perspective on cross-cultural interactions. They reinforced the notion that respect and hospitality can bridge cultural divides and create meaningful connections.

Inviting new and diverse perspectives into your life is a powerful way to widen the lens of your worldview. You'll gain knowledge, uncover new blind spots, and start to see your own life in a more expansive way. In doing so, you'll become well-rounded and better equipped to engage with the wide range of people you'll encounter throughout your leadership journey.

## Have a Growth Mindset

If identifying blind spots and receiving feedback helps you understand where you currently are, then having a growth mindset is what propels you to where you want to go. In her book, *Mindset: The New Psychology of Success*, Carol Dweck emphasizes the importance of adopting a growth mindset over a fixed one:[17]

> "Why waste time proving over and over how great you are, when you could be getting better? Why hide deficiencies instead of overcoming them? Why look for friends or partners who will just shore up your self-esteem instead of ones who will also challenge you to grow? And why seek out the tried and true, instead of experiences that will stretch you? The passion for stretching yourself and sticking to it, even (or especially) when it's not going well, is the hallmark of the growth mindset. This is the mindset that allows people to thrive during some of the most challenging times in their lives."

When you uncover an area for improvement, the most important question is: what are you going to do with that information? With a fixed mindset, you might dismiss it, clinging to your current practices or beliefs even if they are not serving you well. Conversely, with a growth mindset, you see these insights as opportunities to become the person you want to be. Which mindset will you choose to embrace?

## Get Out of Your Comfort Zone

Fortunately, you don't always have to wait to discover a blind spot or receive feedback to develop a growth mindset. You can do this by stepping out of your comfort zone and taking on challenges that have the potential to propel you forward.

In 2011, I traveled for seventeen hours from Los Angeles to Uruguay for a Latin American regional sales conference. I arrived a day early, checked into my hotel, and got a good night's rest. The next morning, I entered the meeting room feeling refreshed and hopeful for the day's sessions. The tables were arranged in a U-shape, ensuring everyone had a clear view of the presenter. In the back, two individuals were ready to provide live translations between English and Spanish. I saw this as a unique opportunity to improve my conversational Spanish, a skill I had developed through my hours volunteering at Shriner's Hospital.

Most of the conference attendees were from Central and South America and spoke Spanish as their first language. While my conversational Spanish was strong, I was more confident discussing business in English. That evening at dinner, my manager asked what language I planned to present in at the meeting. It would be my first time presenting to this group, which included the company's leadership, so I was hesitant to go for it in Spanish. However, I decided to give it a shot.

After the presentation, I received a lot of positive feedback. Although my Spanish was far from perfect, people appreciated the courage and effort I put into it. They also valued hearing the presentation directly from me in their preferred language, rather than through a translation. By exposing my vulnerabilities, I was able to grow and focus on the audience's experience. I had assessed my abilities, seized the opportunity, and trusted that speaking in the language of most attendees would build a stronger connection.

Pushing yourself beyond your comfort zone is crucial for assessing where you are in your journey. We often underestimate our abilities until they are tested. By challenging yourself, you discover what you can truly achieve. I might never have realized that I could make a formal business presentation in Spanish if I hadn't pushed myself. To grow, you must be willing to test the waters and reach beyond your perceived limitations.

## Take Action to Address Shortcomings

Upon joining a medical technology company, I was responsible for implantable devices used to treat brain aneurysms—a dangerous bulge in a blood vessel that can rupture. To prevent this, the aneurysm is often filled with small implants. However, because aneurysms vary in shape and size, it was often unclear which implant sizes would be needed until the surgery was already in progress, requiring hospitals to maintain a comprehensive selection of implants in their inventory. The challenge was that hospitals could not afford to purchase a full assortment upfront due to the high cost.

My team and I began to evaluate a consignment concept as a possible solution for our customers. This involved stocking our implants on the hospital's inventory shelves and billing them only when a specific implant was used, giving hospitals flexibility. While I grasped the logistics behind this arrangement, I struggled to fully understand its business implications, such as how the inventory would impact my company's financials.

This gap in knowledge presented me with a choice. I could continue my current course or take action to improve. Fueled by a growth mindset, I saw pursuing a Master of Business Administration (MBA) degree as a way to increase my business knowledge across many areas, including consignment strategy. It would expose me to the bigger picture of business, expand my network, and equip me with a wealth of insights and skills, making me more effective and successful in my career.

Recognizing this gap in my knowledge and identifying a way to close it, I took action. While continuing to work, I enrolled in the part-time MBA program at the University of California, Irvine. Three years later, I earned my MBA with a whole new perspective.

## Be Honest About Your Limitations

I recently had lunch with a connection I've known for ten years. During our conversation, I mentioned that one of my former colleagues was seeking to expand her network. Since they work in the same field, I asked if he would be open to a networking call with her.

He gladly agreed, and I said I would send an email introduction to them within a few days. After I sent the email, my former colleague replied right away and expressed that she was looking forward to the call. My contact, however, did not reply.

After a week passed, I checked in with him to make sure he had received the introduction. He confirmed that he did and committed to replying to her within a few days. But weeks passed with no communication. He ultimately said that he didn't have the time to meet with her and should never have committed to doing so.

In the busy world we live in, this type of situation is common. People often overcommit themselves and, as a result, fail to follow through on their commitments. Sometimes, they are unaware of their own limitations and commit to something they can't do. If this happens unintentionally, they can say, "I'm sorry. I realize I made a commitment, but I shouldn't have because I don't have the time or the ability to do what I said I would."

Whether you admit your limitations upfront or after realizing you have overcommitted, acknowledging them takes courage. It's hard to admit these things to yourself, and even harder to admit them to others. Yet, showing this vulnerability is not a weakness. It signifies strength and confidence, often earning you more respect as a leader.

## Embrace Vulnerability

Sharing our shortcomings with others and receiving their support can sometimes be all we need to overcome them. Leaders are in a unique position to empower others and embrace their opportunities for improvement. As a leader, you can create this environment by showing your own vulnerability and encouraging others to do the same.

I once worked with Diane, an inspiring leader who excelled at encouraging team members to openly acknowledge their weaknesses and express their growth aspirations. She did this by sharing her own challenges with them. On Diane's team was a less experienced leader, Pete, who was highly respected by his colleagues. However, he had a fear of public speaking, which held him back.

Recognizing Pete's potential, Diane proactively offered him the chance to work with a presentation skills coach to overcome his anxiety. Pete embraced the opportunity, and after several coaching sessions, Diane gave him the spotlight in a team meeting to deliver a critical presentation. His performance was outstanding and drew applause from the entire team.

Watching Pete's growth and success, Diane beamed with pride. Their professional relationship deepened, and Pete's journey inspired others in the group. Seeing him conquer his fears and achieve what once seemed out of reach motivated them to face their own weaknesses and strive for improvement. This ripple effect of growth and shared vulnerability fostered a culture of mutual development and collaboration within the team, reinforcing the importance of knowing where you are and seeking opportunities for growth.

Becoming the leader you aspire to be starts with an honest assessment of your strengths, weaknesses, blind spots, and knowledge gaps. Only then will you be ready to take the next steps and seek opportunities to grow. Whether you're just starting out or well into your journey, maintaining self-awareness is crucial. You can't get to where you want to go without knowing where you currently are. And you can't know where you currently are without self-awareness.

# Exercises

1) Identify two people who know you well and are willing to provide honest feedback. Ask them to give you specific insights about how you come across to others. Record their feedback below.

Feedback from person 1:

Feedback from person 2:

Reflection on feedback:

2) Based on the feedback you received, consider whether there is a gap between how you see yourself and how others see you. Identify the blind spots you'd like to work on and write them down below.

Blind Spot 1:

Blind Spot 2:

Blind Spot 3:

## CHAPTER FIVE

# A MENSCH CULTIVATES THEIR CIRCLE

The people who are the happiest and the healthiest and the most fulfilled, are the people who make it a practice—an ongoing practice—to attend to their relationships.

Dr. Robert Waldinger

In the spring, when a new growing season begins, a farmer spends hundreds of hours getting their fields ready. They put significant effort and resources into planting new crops, even though they can't see the seeds yet. After a few weeks, tiny sprouts start to appear, showing the first signs of life. This is when the farmer begins to see their hard work pay off. But their job isn't done yet. To enjoy a bountiful harvest in the fall, they need to keep nurturing and taking care of the crops.

Relationships are no different. Like the farmer's crop, they require ongoing energy and attention. Personal relationships with family and friends often develop without conscious effort. You might mark your mother-in-law's birthday on your calendar to remember to get her a gift or call your spouse after lunch to ask about their morning presentation. We all know that the more effort we put into these relationships, the stronger they become.

However, it is easy to forget that professional relationships need the same care and attention to make a difference in our careers. A mensch understands this and, like the farmer, takes the time to nurture their professional circle. There is a common saying in the business world: it's not *what* you know, but *who* you know. I've experienced firsthand just how true this is throughout my life.

In the summer of 2002, my wife, Mindy, and I had been married for a little under a year. We were living with my two brothers in a three-bedroom apartment near Fenway Park. Although we had deep ties to Boston and enjoyed rooting for the Red Sox, we had grown tired of city life and cold winters. Eager for a fresh start in a warmer climate and our own place, we planned a vacation to the West Coast, starting with three days in Las Vegas, where we visited close friends. After sharing our thoughts about moving, they suggested we consider Southern California. Coincidentally, our next stop on the trip was Orange County, located between Los Angeles and San Diego, which we quickly fell in love with.

During our visit to California, the sun came out every day, and the temperature was perfect. We spent most of our time at or near the beach, enjoying the scenery and the relaxing vibe. One afternoon, we picked up take-out from a popular local seafood restaurant. We ate our lunch on the beach and asked a lifeguard what else we might do that afternoon. He said, "You have the ocean, sand volleyball down the beach, and plenty of restaurants and shops on the boardwalk. What more could you ask for?" Mindy and I looked at each other and knew we were thinking the same thing.

When we returned to Boston, we were focused on making a move to Southern California. I had been with a small startup company for the past year, but the company was struggling financially, and I knew I wouldn't be there much longer. I booked a flight to Orange County for six weeks later, setting up as many meetings and interviews as possible in hopes of securing a job to facilitate our move.

I started by researching life sciences companies in Southern California and identified those that interested me. Every day, I sent emails, made phone calls, and wrote letters to people at my target companies. I contacted recruiters and reached out to former classmates, coworkers, and industry contacts, asking for any connections they had at these companies.

My former boss, Amy, was my manager when I was working part-time while studying at Boston University. She supported my job search by connecting me with one of her contacts in Southern California, who helped arrange some meetings. Amy also wrote me a recommendation letter that ultimately helped me land a job. In 2002, the job market was weak, and the economy had been in a recession for over a year. It was not an ideal time to be job hunting, but with the support of my network and mensches like Amy, I was able to navigate the challenging job market effectively. With their guidance and introductions, I managed to secure a series of promising interviews. By the time six weeks rolled around, I had a full schedule lined up. With Mindy's well wishes, I was off.

During that week-long trip, I stayed with my cousin, whose house was within walking distance of the beach. Every morning, I walked along the water, which helped clear my head as I prepared for my meetings. One particularly important appointment was with

Michael, then the CEO of a growing medical device company in Orange County. Having come across his name during my research, I remembered him as one of the investment partners at the startup where I recently worked. Our interactions had always been positive, and he was happy to meet with me. Although his company didn't have any openings for me at the time, he provided insights into the local industry and interview tips, which helped me during the rest of my visit.

A couple weeks after that whirlwind trip, I was hired by a medical device company, where I spent three rewarding years. The effort I put in over those six weeks, leveraging my existing relationships and building new ones, led to a significant turning point in both my personal and professional life.

Of course, such efforts are not easy. It takes courage to put yourself out there, along with dedication and self-confidence. Not all your efforts will pan out. Some may lead to dead ends, and that's okay. But if you keep at it, the connections you make and the relationships you build will be invaluable throughout your journey.

## The Essence of Networking

Contrary to popular belief, networking isn't about reaching out to people only when you need a favor. Building a productive network requires years of effort and planning. Like a farmer who tends to their crops early to ensure a good harvest, you must nurture your relationships long before you need them. When I was looking for a new job in California, I relied on relationships I had built years earlier.

That being said, not every relationship is meant to last forever. As I explained to my two children, when they lost contact with a friend who moved away, people come in and out of our lives. Some, like family, stay for a long time, while others are present only briefly. If we're lucky, they teach us valuable lessons and enrich our lives, and we hopefully do the same for them. It's natural for some relationships to eventually end. However, there are certain relationships that are important to hold onto and develop. A mensch recognizes this and makes the necessary effort to maintain them.

Also, not all relationships need to be strong. In his book *Give and Take: Why Helping Others Drives Our Success*, Adam Grant writes "Strong ties are our close friends and colleagues, the people we really trust. Weak ties are our acquaintances, the people we know casually." We each have a mix of "strong" and "weak" relationships in our lives. When cultivating our network, we often assume that only strong relationships have value. Yet, a study summarized by Grant found that "people were significantly more likely to benefit from weak ties… Strong ties provide bonds, but weak ties serve as bridges: they provide more efficient access to new information. Our strong ties tend to travel in the same social circles and know about the same opportunities as we do. Weak ties are more likely to open up access to a different network, facilitating the discovery of original leads."[18] It's important to remember that even weak connections can bring value to your life. Don't neglect them or underestimate their power.

Throughout my career, even as I've moved on from one company to another, I have always tried to stay connected to former colleagues, relationships which might be considered weak.

For example, I have a dedicated calendar with their birthdays and make it a point to reach out with birthday wishes every year. This small action keeps our relationship going with no strings attached. I don't expect to ever need something from them. I simply feel that our relationship adds value to both our lives, so it is worth keeping in touch.

A mensch doesn't expand their network solely for potential future benefits. Instead, they do so because it enriches their own life and the lives of others, fostering a sense of community. By maintaining these connections, a mensch creates a web of relationships that build a foundation of trust and goodwill. This approach not only strengthens personal and professional bonds but also contributes to a more connected and supportive world.

So, how do you cultivate your crop of relationships and people that will support your path before you even know what that path might be? The good news is that connecting with others is much easier now than it was in the past. Professional associations and tools like LinkedIn simplify finding and contacting people with whom you might want to develop a relationship. If you're not already using these resources, take some time to familiarize yourself with them. See the exercises at the end of this chapter for suggestions.

Once you know how to connect with others, the question becomes, with whom do you connect? Most of us have no problem developing relationships with coworkers, mentors, clients, and other industry contacts. But if you limit your efforts to this first level of network-building, you might find that your circle is quite small and lacks diversity. A mensch, on the other hand, will build their network by stepping outside of their immediate bubble.

By exploring new industries and meeting different people, you not only open yourself up to new ideas and potential new opportunities, but also enhance your ability to support others. This proactive approach fosters a diverse, robust network that can offer fresh perspectives, valuable insights, and unexpected opportunities.

## Protect Your Network

My mother always reminded me and my brothers that the world is very small. You never know who will remember you, or more importantly, *how* they will remember you. A mensch understands that how you conduct yourself directly impacts your relationships and the strength of your network.

At the first company that I joined after moving to California, one of the senior leaders emphasized the company's values, particularly integrity. He shared something that stood out to me: imagine you go about your day with a camera and microphone mounted on you. Then, at the end of the day, your friends and family watch and listen to everything you said and did. How would you feel about your actions? Would your loved ones be proud? Integrity is about always doing the right thing, whether anyone is watching.

A couple of years ago, a former coworker, Melissa, was laid off from her decades-long job. Melissa and I weren't in the same department, but we often collaborated on different projects. When we first started working together, she was friendly and supportive, but over time, she became distant and cold. I never understood why our relationship changed.

When I heard about her layoff, memories of our strained past surfaced, but I chose to remember the early days when our relationship was strong. Motivated by these positive memories, I reached out to her, offering to write a recommendation and make introductions to key contacts. I wasn't sure how she would respond, but she replied with gratitude and expressed her surprise at my offer to help. A few days later, I sent her a glowing recommendation that she could use in her job search. She reached out to thank me, saying that my support had boosted her confidence during a tough time. Before long, she was hired by a new company.

This experience reminded me how powerful a little kindness can be. Even when relationships change or drift apart, being there for someone can make a huge difference. It reinforced that keeping those connections alive, even if they're not perfect, can lead to great things.

As your career takes you through various twists and turns, it is important to remember that your network is an asset. Besides growing it, you must also protect it. One key way to do this is by maintaining a positive reputation, which you achieve by acting with integrity and kindness—by being a mensch.

Just as a healthy network can support you along your professional path, it can also impact your personal life. Mindy and I would have never met if it hadn't been for our social network. In 1998, Mindy's sister, Jill, set her up on a blind date with Jill's friend's brother, Brad, who happened to be a good friend of mine. Brad lived a couple of hours away and came to Boston to meet Mindy on a Saturday night. There were no sparks on their date, but since they had already made plans to go to a food festival the following afternoon, he invited me to come along. That's when I met Mindy. I felt a special connection to her right away and asked her out on a date later that week after clearing it with Brad. She invited me to join her and some of her friends for dinner at a small Italian restaurant the following weekend. I showed up, and the rest is history. Had it not been for Mindy's sister, her friend, Kim, and our broader social network, our paths might never have crossed. The point is, you never know where your relationships and network might lead you.

## The Power of Human Connection

It's clear that having strong relationships can result in positive outcomes both personally and professionally. However, a mensch doesn't build relationships for personal gain. A mensch understands that the relationship itself is valuable. Research has shown that relationships significantly impact our overall health and happiness.

Humans are social creatures, and the connections we form with others fulfill one of our most basic human needs. According to psychologist Abraham Maslow, who developed the human hierarchy of needs, our most basic ones are physiological, including food, water, warmth, and rest. Next is our need for safety. Once these are met, we have psychological needs, including a sense of belongingness filled by relationships and human connection.

The Harvard Study of Adult Development, the longest-running study on human happiness, has tracked the lives of thousands of people across multiple generations, evaluating numerous factors that contribute to health, happiness, and longevity. In their summary of the findings, the directors of the study stated: "Through all the years of studying these lives, one crucial factor stands out for the consistency and power of its ties to physical health, mental health, and longevity. Contrary to what many people might think, it's not career achievement, or exercise, or a healthy diet. Don't get us wrong; these things matter. But one thing continuously demonstrates its broad and enduring importance: good relationships. In fact, close personal connections are significant enough that if we had to take all eighty-five years of the Harvard Study and boil it down to a single principle for living, one life investment that is supported by similar findings across a variety of other studies, it would be this: Good relationships keep us healthier and happier. Period."[19]

Dr. Robert Waldinger, one of the study's directors, further emphasized these findings in an episode of *The Ed Mylett Show*, where he described the concept of "social fitness." He pointed out how we are all familiar with the concept of physical fitness, which requires a commitment of time and energy. Our social fitness, he explained, is no different. The people who are the happiest in this world are those who make caring for their relationships a purposeful practice.[20]

While relationships have a clear impact on our happiness, they also tend to be what matters most at the end of our careers. When you look back, you are unlikely to recall the specifics of a project or task that you completed. What you will remember, though, are the relationships you had and how they made you feel.

In 2016, I was on the executive leadership team when my company decided to acquire a smaller company. The acquisition brought cutting-edge technology that would help us achieve our growth goals by making us first-to-market in a new area of the industry. The smaller company also had a culture that was complementary to ours. Our CEO, Rich, valued the people and didn't want anyone to lose their jobs just because of the acquisition. Instead, he supported us in finding roles for the incoming employees—roughly one hundred people. Rich was committed to taking care of the business and the people. In the end, we integrated nearly all of them and exceeded our financial targets and continued to do so in the years that followed.

A couple of years later at the same company, a colleague faced a sudden medical condition that required her to take an extended leave of absence from work. When Rich heard about the employee's situation, he personally made sure that she and her family received the benefits and support they needed.

I met with Rich for coffee shortly after I began writing this book and was excited to listen to his thoughts on leadership. I asked him what his greatest achievement was as a leader. Rich answered that it was the culture he built and the relationships he established while building a highly successful company. Throughout his career, he prioritized people and did so without seeking recognition. Rich thoroughly understands the importance of human connection and doing good for others. As author and speaker Simon Sinek points out in *Leaders Eat Last*, this makes Rich unique. "Sadly, it is more common for leaders of companies to see the people as the means to drive numbers. [Great leaders] do not see people as a commodity to be managed to help grow the money. They see the money as the commodity to be managed to help grow the people."[21]

Some of the most rewarding connections I've made have come from my travels. I've been fortunate to visit thirty-five countries, some multiple times, and each trip exposed me to different cultures, unique landscapes, and many delicious meals. Yet oftentimes, shortly after the trip and sometimes just the next day, I can't recall the name of a building, a historical fact, or even what I ate the previous night. What always stays with me, though, are the special experiences and conversations I had with people. Like the drink I had at an outdoor pub with my former colleague in Hamburg, Germany. I can't remember what type of beer we had that afternoon, but I will always remember the lively conversation we had about our families and hobbies while looking at the aircraft manufacturing plant in the distance.

From a conference I attended in Cape Town, South Africa, roughly fifteen years ago, I don't remember what topics were covered in the meetings, but I will always remember the fantastic bus tour I took with a colleague and the lunch we had by the ocean that day. The combination of breathtaking scenery, engaging conversation, and the sound of the waves made it an unforgettable experience.

During my MBA program, one Friday night really stands out. I was part of a six-person team, and we were working on a big presentation that had to be delivered the next morning. As the deadline crept closer, we could all feel the pressure. We had our disagreements, but we trusted each other and kept pushing forward. By the time midnight rolled around, we were all exhausted, surviving on caffeine and a pizza we had delivered. I don't remember much about the actual presentation or even what it was about, but I'll never forget how we worked through the stress and challenges together until 2:00 a.m. We cracked jokes when we needed a break, shared stories about our lives, and gave each other the energy to keep going. That sense of camaraderie, the feeling that we had each other's backs, is what really stuck with me. In moments like that you realize it's not the work itself that makes a lasting impression—it's the people you meet and the connections you build along the way.

If you're in the early stages of your career, this is a great time to begin cultivating your network. Be the farmer who's clearing the field and watering the seeds. Be a mensch who builds a level of social fitness and maintains valuable relationships. If you're further along your path and are feeling stuck, try revisiting your network. It's never too late to reach out to past contacts or make new ones. Doing so is a great way to breathe more life into your journey. Treat your relationships as the priceless asset that they are. When you act like a mensch and do the right thing just for the sake of doing the right thing, you will inevitably cultivate a valuable circle and build a foundation that will support you along your journey.

# Exercises

1) Reconnect with Your Network.

   Identify two people from your network whom you haven't been in touch with recently but believe it would be beneficial to reconnect with (e.g., a former colleague). Consider how you can offer support to them and how they might be able to support you.

   Person 1.
   - Name:
   - How you can support them:
   - How they might support you:

   Person 2.
   - Name:
   - How you can support them:
   - How they might support you:

   Maintain Regular Contact.

   Identify at least one specific action you can take to maintain regular contact with each of these people (e.g., sending annual birthday greetings, scheduling a monthly coffee meeting). Then, implement a system to ensure you follow through on these actions (e.g., setting calendar reminders).

Person 1:
- Action:
- Accountability method:

Person 2:
- Action:
- Accountability method:

2) Connect with Second-Degree Connections on LinkedIn. Use LinkedIn search filters to identify three second-degree connections in your network who you would like to meet, considering the value of diversifying your circle. Reach out to your mutual first-degree connection to request an introduction or send a personalized invitation to the second-degree connection explaining why you'd like to connect. Once you are connected, follow up to arrange a virtual or in-person meeting to explore how you can support each other in your respective journeys.

Connection 1:
- Name:
- Approach:
- Follow-up plan:

Connection 2:
- Name:
- Approach:
- Follow-up plan:

Connection 3:
- Name:
- Approach:
- Follow-up plan:


3) Research industry associations within your current field or a new industry you wish to explore. Compile a list of upcoming conferences or events hosted by these associations that you might find valuable to attend. Consider how these events can enhance your knowledge and expand your professional network.

Industry Association 1:
- Name:
- Upcoming Event:
- Date and Location:
- Reason for attending:

Industry Association 2:
- Name:
- Upcoming Event:
- Date and Location:
- Reason for attending:

# CHAPTER SIX

# A MENSCH PUTS IN THE WORK

Those times when you get up early and you work hard, those times when you stay up late and you work hard, those times when you don't feel like working, you're too tired, you don't want to push yourself, but you do it anyway. That is actually the dream.

Kobe Bryant

When I was a kid in the 1980s, I loved watching "the big game:" the epic basketball matchups between the Boston Celtics and the Los Angeles Lakers. These teams played each other twice every season, once in Boston and once in Los Angeles. It was the biggest rivalry in the NBA, perhaps in all professional sports. Larry Bird of the Celtics and Magic Johnson of the Lakers were the standout players on each team and had competed against each other in college before entering the NBA as rookies the same year. Larry played at Indiana State University and Magic at Michigan State University, and their schools faced off in the 1979 national championship game, which remains the highest-rated TV college basketball game in history. Magic and the Spartans won 75-64.

The thrilling games between them continued until 1991 when Magic announced to the public that he was HIV positive.

Many feared he would soon become very sick and die. Over the following years, he retired from and returned to basketball several times. Most importantly, he continued living a successful and happy life, still going strong more than thirty years after his diagnosis.

After decades of following his career and story, I had the chance to listen to Magic speak in person about his journey growing up, playing professional basketball, facing obstacles as an HIV-positive person, and succeeding as a leader in the community and business world. He shared valuable insights on resilience, the importance of a positive attitude, and the power of giving back. His words were as inspiring as his career, and I was as in awe of him at sixty-two years old as I had been when he was a young basketball player.

In 1996, just five years after Magic's retirement, another basketball legend emerged when eighteen-year-old Kobe Bryant joined the Los Angeles Lakers. Kobe went on to become one of the greatest players ever. But as much natural skill as Kobe had, he also possessed something else: an extraordinary work ethic. His work ethic became so recognized and appreciated by fans that it was coined the "Mamba Mentality," after Kobe's nickname, The Black Mamba, which he gave himself to represent his assassin-like persona on the basketball court.

When Kobe tragically died in a helicopter crash at age forty-one in 2020, basketball fans lost one of the greatest players of all time. But even more importantly, the world lost a man who epitomized the definition of hard work. Despite the tragedy, something uplifting happened in the aftermath. When his former teammates, coaches, and the media spoke about Kobe's life, they first noted his success as a basketball player. But each also recognized his unmatched work ethic, almost as much as his success.

## The Unseen Hours

The world of professional sports is filled with talented individuals who work hard day in and day out, commit to their goals, and accept the grind, especially when no one is watching. In the book *Raise Your Game*, authors Allen Stein Jr. and Jon Sternfeld discuss the concept of "unseen hours," a phrase coined by basketball skills coach Drew Hanlen. Unseen hours refer to the effort one spends fine-tuning their craft, specifically while no one is watching, to perform at their best for a short period that is often seen by others. For professional athletes, these unseen hours are key to success. While you might not spend hours alone in a gym perfecting your free throw, your unseen hours are just as important. The level of commitment and effort you consistently put in makes all the difference.

The mindset you bring to your unseen hours is a matter of self-discipline. Do you ease off the gas and put in less effort when no one is watching? Or do you dig deep and bring your best? To reach your goals or become the leader you aspire to be, you must hold yourself accountable.

## Do the Best You Can Every Day

In his book *The Attributes*, bestselling author and retired Navy SEAL Commander Rich Diviney explains his preference for the term "optimal performance" over "peak performance."[22] While most people tout peak performance as the ultimate goal, Diviney argues that achieving your absolute peak—the very best you are capable of—is not feasible every single day. Various factors, such as health and other circumstances, can impact your capabilities. For example, if you come down with the flu, your productivity will likely decrease. If a natural disaster strikes, plans and opportunities will be interrupted.

Striving for optimal performance, however, accounts for these variables and provides a more realistic goal. Instead of pressuring yourself to always perform at your absolute best, focus on putting in your best effort. The mensch method embraces this mindset, emphasizing the importance of doing your best with integrity, even when circumstances aren't ideal. It's about meeting yourself where you are on any given day and not getting caught up in chasing perfection. Life can be unpredictable, and things like getting sick, stress, or other unforeseen challenges will inevitably come up. What matters is how you respond to these challenges and move forward in a way that reflects your values and commitment.

Effort and consistency go a long way, even when things aren't perfect. Life will always throw some curveballs but making sure that you're giving your best—regardless of the outcome—helps you manage stress and keeps you moving forward.

In 2002, I had just started a new job at a medical device company in California and was participating in a rigorous three-week training program there. During this time, Mindy was back in Massachusetts, finishing up the packing for our move to California. I hoped for some flexibility to help us settle into our new home, but I quickly realized that wouldn't be the case.

On my first day, I met my fellow training class colleagues and listened to an inspiring introduction from one of the company's leaders. We also received homework that, while not difficult, was very time-consuming. The next day, I noticed a few newly vacant seats in the classroom, and by the following afternoon, three more seats were empty. I soon realized that these absences were due to some of my colleagues not meeting the company's high expectations. I felt a mix of stress and determination, understanding that I needed to rise to meet the company's high standards while balancing the demands of the training with the responsibilities of our move.

Mindy encouraged me to keep doing my best, reminding me that all I could control was my attitude and effort. Her advice really helped me get through those tough weeks. It was a lot to juggle, with training sessions that stretched my limits while we were preparing to relocate. By focusing on what I could control—my own effort and how I responded to the stress—I made it through. At the end of the three-week program, 75 percent of us graduated, and I felt accomplished, not because I had been perfect, but because I didn't let up.

This experience reinforced a key principle: it's not about always performing at your peak; it's about showing up and doing your best. Top athletes like LeBron James know the importance of putting in their best effort even it if means they don't score the most points. In the same way, I've found that whether I'm working out or preparing for a meeting, what really matters is the effort I put in.

This applies across all areas of life. Whether you're dealing with a big project at work or just going through the motions of a daily routine, your attitude and effort shape the results of your actions.

This mindset, which is core to the mensch method, is about maintaining high standards and being consistent, even when things aren't going perfectly. It's the little things—showing up, putting in the work—that accumulate over time and lead to bigger successes. By staying consistent, even on the tough days, you're creating ripples that spread out and affect all the other areas of your life.

In the end, it's not about chasing perfection or expecting yourself to always be at your absolute best. It's about committing to the process, doing what you can each day, and knowing that those efforts will add up. This kind of consistency is what it means to live as a mensch—showing up with integrity, effort, and purpose, regardless of the obstacles. That's how we build the kind of life and career that's grounded in values, rather than short-lived bursts of achievement.

## Compete with Yourself

Two years before his death, Kobe Bryant released his book, *The Mamba Mentality*. He described the Mamba Mentality as "simply trying to be the best version of yourself. That's what the mentality means. Every day you're trying to become better."[23] In essence, Kobe was highlighting the effort to move your optimal performance closer to your peak performance, gradually aligning what you achieve on an average day with what you are capable of on your very best day. This journey is fueled by the effort you invest during the unseen hours and is a competition with no one but yourself.

When our kids, Alex and Marina, were young, Mindy and I enrolled them in a community swimming program. The team had typical meets where swimmers raced against each other in their respective strokes, but there was something unique about this program. Instead of focusing on the fastest swimmer in each heat, the format encouraged each individual swimmer to beat their own time. The swimmers who improved against their personal best received formal recognition that day. Coaches, teammates, and parents all supported the swimmers as you would expect in any other competition. As a parent, I embraced this model and the lessons it taught my children. Not only did they learn to swim, but they also learned an important lesson about self-improvement.

Competition against and comparison to others is ingrained in modern culture and is the foundation of our school system and corporate industries in the United States. Too often, you might find yourself overly focused on comparing yourself to your peers at work such as who has the best title or salary, or even the best parking spot. You can find yourself struggling to "keep up with the Joneses" in your neighborhood and social circles. This unhealthy focus is something you must strive to unlearn.

The rise of social media has made this issue even worse, bringing a whole new level of pressure and comparison into our daily lives. Take my friend Daniel, for example. He found himself caught up in negative self-talk because he felt intimidated by the false impressions of a stranger on social media. This kind of exposure can undermine your ability to be your best. Constantly seeing stories of others' seemingly perfect lives can make you question the value of your own efforts and feel inadequate.

However, the competition that matters most—the one that drives you to be your personal best—is the competition with yourself. You are on your own journey. What's important is the progress you make toward your own goals, becoming the leader you aspire to be, and being a mensch along the way. Concerning yourself with what your neighbor is doing is a distraction at best and a deterrent at worst. Stay in your own lane and focus on achieving your personal best.

## Hold to Your Standards

Two-time Super Bowl-winning head coach, Mike Tomlin, is known for his coaching philosophy that emphasizes consistency and accountability. He sums it up with the expression, "The standard is the standard." It's a simple yet powerful rule, implying that whatever standard you set for yourself, you must stick to it. Unlike a goal, which you might or might not achieve, a standard is an expectation for how you do something. It's almost always in your control and can be achieved 100 percent of the time.

For example, the goal of most professional football teams each year is to win the Super Bowl. However, with thirty-two teams in the National Football League, thirty-one of them will not do it. Their standard, on the other hand, could be that everyone on the team exercises in the weight room every day from 6:00 to 8:00 in the morning or runs twenty sprints at the end of each practice. These standards set the expectation for daily effort and commitment, regardless of the outcome.

Over the past several years, I've consciously worked toward living a healthier, more balanced life. When I started on this journey, I didn't set any specific health-related goals such as losing a certain number of pounds or achieving a specific resting heart rate. Instead, I set standards for myself. I committed to waking up every morning at six, exercising, working hard, and feeding my mind, body, and soul with positivity—whether through the books I read, the people I meet, or the projects I work on. This practice didn't drastically change my life overnight, but by consistently sticking to the standards I set, I have managed to achieve a healthy and balanced lifestyle.

Adhering to your standards also means remaining committed no matter what. Even when you don't feel like doing something, you need to do it because the standard you set for yourself is non-negotiable. For example, I have a standard to work out five mornings per week for at least forty-five minutes. Sometimes, I wake up and just don't feel like driving to the gym for such a tough workout. However, because the standard I set for myself trumps my feelings, I always get in the car and workout anyway. I feel better after completing it, especially on the days I don't feel like going.

When I am at the gym, I also have a standard to never quit. Once I start the workout, I finish it. I focus on completing each repetition and staying true to my standards by working through the challenge. Successfully facing such challenges reminds me of what Steve Magness describes in *Do Hard Things:* "Real toughness is experiencing discomfort or distress, leaning in, paying attention, and creating space to take thoughtful action."[24] Magness's definition of toughness is the ability to hold to your standards even when facing adversity.

To fully embody the mensch method, it's about more than just sticking to your standards when things are going well; it's about staying committed to what you've set out to do, even when it's difficult. Living by this method isn't just about setting and following standards—it's about upholding those standards through challenges while being mindful of how your actions affect others. By maintaining accountability and consistency in your actions, you not only stay true to your values but also create a positive impact on those around you. A powerful tool to help you do this is a personal identity statement.

## Your Personal Identity Statement

Dr. Jason Selk, a renowned performance coach and former Director of Sports Psychology for the St. Louis Cardinals baseball team, highlights the power of a personal identity statement. It's something you can lean on during stressful or challenging times to remind yourself of who you are and why you're committed to what you're doing. This statement should reflect your unique identity and be aspirational, embodying who you want to become. Having a personal identity statement also helps you stay focused and silence negative self-talk.

When I'm at the gym pushing through a tough workout or preparing to give a presentation, I think about my statement: "I am a loving father, husband, brother, uncle, son, and friend. I always show up for others, follow through on my commitments, and am kind to myself and others. I am happy, healthy, confident, strong, inspiring, honest, authentic, and grateful." Depending on what challenge I'm facing, I draw on different parts of this statement to remind me of my values, standards, and why I'm putting in the effort. My personal identity statement gives me a motivational boost and keeps me disciplined, especially during the unseen hours.

What I appreciate most about Selk's perspective is his observation that "you will neither outperform nor underperform your self-image for long."[25] The idea is that if you have a clear statement and are committed to it, you'll naturally perform close to that target. Your personal identity statement will shape who you become, so develop it wisely. Make sure it strikes the right balance between being aspirational and realistic, challenging yet attainable.

## Prioritize Balance

A mensch always gives their best effort and works hard during the unseen hours. But to keep delivering their optimal performance, a mensch also takes care of their physical and mental health. There is a fine line between effort and exhaustion, and the key to avoiding burnout is to deliberately maintain balance.

Take Simone Biles, the world's most decorated gymnast, as an example. Her remarkable success came from countless unseen hours of hard work and dedication. But in 2021, at the Tokyo Summer Olympics, something unexpected happened. Shortly before the team competition, Biles pulled out. Initially citing an injury, she later explained that she was not in a healthy mental state and needed to prioritize her mental health. The public was divided between applauding Biles and criticizing her, debating over the pressure felt by an Olympic athlete. However, it is never our place to judge someone else's experience. What cannot be debated is that burnout can affect anyone, whether Olympic athletes or people like you and me.

After a two-year hiatus, Simone Biles returned in 2023 and performed as powerfully as ever, winning the all-around gold at the World Championships. The following year, at the Paris Summer Olympics, she continued her dominance by winning the gold medal in the all-around competition and a total of four medals during the games. Her triumphant return demonstrated that prioritizing balance and health is not an automatic path to failure. In fact, the opposite is often true. If you push too hard for too long, you risk burnout. Your journey is a marathon, not a sprint. To maintain optimal performance, a mensch prioritizes balance. The reason is simple: when you are balanced, you are healthy—mind, body, and soul. And when you are at your healthiest, you can perform closest to your peak.

## Effort Leads to Growth

In Chapter 4, you saw how having a growth mindset is crucial for moving forward on your journey. The story of the presentation I gave in Spanish showed how stepping outside your comfort zone can help you discover your limitations and push yourself further.

It's tempting to stick to what you're good at and stay comfortable there. However, as your abilities and performance improve over time, it is important not to get complacent and let your efforts plateau. Even if you achieve your greatest potential in one area, trying something entirely new can be beneficial. It allows you to diversify your skills, prevents burnout, and makes you even stronger on your journey.

The key is not to get so comfortable that you stop putting in effort. A mensch constantly looks for ways to improve, whether by moving their optimal performance closer to their peak or by diversifying their goals and interests. Having something to work for drives a mensch toward success and fulfillment.

On my own growth journey, every step forward involved trying something new and stepping out of my comfort zone. I believe that's where true growth happens. As a leader, my philosophy is to create an environment that encourages people to improve and challenge themselves. To do this, they need to try things they haven't done before, which might lead to mistakes. However, these mistakes are part of the learning process. As a mensch, you can guide people through their learning journey, helping them avoid repeating the same mistakes. As long as they are learning and growing, that's what matters.

In 2007, when I was not selected for the top talent employees' program, I made a choice. Rather than accepting their opinion of me, I got out of my comfort zone and put in the work. Seven years later, I was a senior executive at a major medical technology company and a respected leader in the industry.

To move from who you are today to who you want to become, you must be willing to put in the work. The hours you spend striving to improve yourself—the hours that no one else sees—that effort, that commitment, is what leads you down the road of personal growth and success. While it is unrealistic to expect peak performance every day, giving your best and holding yourself to the standards you've set are keys to reaching your ultimate goals.

# Exercises

Crafting Your Personal Identity Statement.

1) Identify three elements you want to include in your personal identity statement, considering who you are and who you aspire to become:

a)

b)

c)

2) Using the above elements as input, draft a personal identity statement.

3) What is one specific action you can start doing today to move toward your personal or professional goals? Use the SMART criteria (Specific, Measurable, Achievable, Relevant, and Time-bound).

## CHAPTER SEVEN

# A MENSCH TAKES CARE OF THEMSELF

Keep your face always toward the sunshine, and shadows will fall behind you.

Walt Whitman

When my primary care physician of fifteen years retired a few years ago, I had my first appointment with my new doctor. He began by asking how I was feeling. I told him that I felt mentally and physically as strong as ever. He said it was great to hear and asked me to explain why I felt this way. I shared my daily practices and how I had integrated them into my life. He responded by telling me that I could be the spokesperson for his practice. He explained that too many people of a similar age are overly stressed, have high blood pressure, are depressed, and feel trapped in their lives without seeing a path out. Unfortunately, they make little effort to change their circumstances, not realizing it is within their power to improve their lives. But with a mensch mindset, a healthy lifestyle is entirely possible.

## Happiness Leads to Success

In *The Happiness Advantage*, Shawn Achor challenges society's perception of happiness. He argues that happiness leads to success, not the other way around. Today's society—through schools, workplaces, and even the way we consume—teaches us that accomplishments are what make us happy. As a result, we're always chasing "success," thinking it will eventually lead us to happiness.

However, Achor and other researchers have discovered that the connection actually works the other way around. A mensch is someone who finds happiness in their life, no matter how much outward success they have. Ironically, this happiness tends to lead to outward success, creating a self-fulfilling prophecy. Conversely, those who seek happiness through external achievements may never really feel fulfilled.

This concept is challenging though because the idea that success leads to happiness is deeply ingrained in us. So, how do we find happiness without depending on success? The answer lies in our mindset.

## The Power of Positive Thinking

In *Raise Your Game*, Stein and Sternfeld describe the power of shifting your mindset from "have to" to "get to." For example, balancing multiple projects means you get to take on many challenges and grow in your career. In my case, instead of thinking, "I have to attend this networking event," I began telling myself, "I get to expand my professional network and explore new opportunities," valuing the connections I can make.

After many months of intentionally shifting my mindset from "have to" to "get to," I noticed I started becoming more grateful for all the blessings in my life. The more of them I noticed, the more they seemed to appear. Similarly, when I changed my thinking to embrace the happiness I already had in my life, this led me to success. Once I stopped chasing outward accomplishment in search of happiness, happiness simply found me.

About six months into my new "get to" lifestyle, I was finishing up a workout when someone approached me. He mentioned that he had noticed my hard work at the gym over the past several months and expressed his admiration for my commitment. When he asked about my physical transformation, I explained that I was on a journey to improve my overall lifestyle, starting with a few incremental changes and being diligent about them every day. When he asked how much weight I had lost, I answered that I had no idea because I hadn't weighed myself. I told him that my measure of success was not my weight, but how I felt. Viewing my exercise routine as something I get to do each day made it possible. I wasn't withholding happiness from myself until I reached a certain number on the scale. Just the experience of taking care of my body made me feel good. This approach led me to even more success on my health journey, which resulted in me losing weight anyway.

## Small Changes Lead to Big Results

In *Good to Great*, Jim Collins introduces the concept of the flywheel.[26] Imagine a large, heavy metal wheel mounted on an axle.

You have a goal to get the wheel moving in one particular direction. Where do you begin? You take a deep breath, step up, and pull. The initial movements are so small that they may be imperceptible. But right away, you reach up and pull again. The wheel shows slightly more movement than it did after the first pull. If you are consistent and patient, after many minutes of pulling, the wheel will begin to circle around at full speed. Eventually, the wheel gains enough momentum to keep turning on its own.

What I find most compelling about Collins' analogy is that you can't pinpoint which pull made the wheel start moving on its own. Incremental change is not about a precise set of steps where one specific effort makes all the difference. Success results from a series of consistent efforts, no matter how small.

Collins presents the flywheel concept in the context of organizations growing or changing, moving toward a certain objective ("greatness"). He points out that companies implementing over-the-top initiatives rarely see results, when compared to organizations that commit to small changes over an extended period. They start out pulling the flywheel with an exorbitant amount of effort, burning out too quickly. Or they lack the patience to make enough small pulls and decide to stop and try a different approach. While Collins is describing corporate journeys, the concept is also applicable to anyone's journey. When implemented in a dedicated and consistent manner, even small efforts can lead to big results.

In *Atomic Habits*, James Clear explains the power of these deliberate, small changes. "Every action you take is a vote for the type of person you wish to become. No single instance will transform your beliefs, but as the votes build up, so does the evidence of your new identity. This is one reason why meaningful change does not require radical change. Small habits can make a meaningful difference by providing evidence of a new identity. And if a change is meaningful, it is actually big. That's the paradox of making small improvements."[27]

Not only do small changes feel easier to tackle, but they are often more effective in the long run. Consider the tradition of New Year's resolutions, which usually involve drastic lifestyle changes simply because it is a new year. However, this approach often fails to achieve lasting change. True change comes from making small shifts on any given day of the year because you want to move closer to who you aspire to be, not just because it happens to be January 1.

While I completely value the process of understanding where you are and where you want to go, making significant changes should not be reserved only for the beginning of the year. Changes also do not have to be drastic. You are more likely to achieve your goals if the changes you make are small and sustainable. In *Streaking to Win*, author Andre Julian emphasizes this by referring to it as wiring yourself for success. He writes, "Micro-goal setting works because we really need to get rewarded with small steps along the way when we are marching toward a larger goal."[28] Implementing changes throughout the year, rather than overwhelming yourself with major resolutions, can lead to more consistent and meaningful progress.

## Staying Balanced

When you're pulling the flywheel to achieve your goals, it's easy to overexert yourself and burn out. A mensch understands the importance of pacing themselves along the journey and maintaining balance.

There are several steps you can take to remain balanced while giving your optimal performance each day. The first is to make sure that when you invest significant effort, you are doing so because you want to, not because someone else demands it. You might be performing for the benefit of others, and that's fine, as long as you *want* to perform for them. Author and former palliative care worker, Bronnie Ware, details in *The Top Five Regrets of the Dying* that the regret she heard most often from those in her care during their last days was, "I wish I'd had the courage to live a life true to myself, not the life others expected of me."[29] Performing solely for others adds a lot of pressure and can eliminate intrinsic motivation, making that flywheel heavier with every pull.

The next step to achieving balance is to recognize and respect your physical and mental limits, which vary greatly from person to person. For example, a professional athlete may be able to play on a sprained ankle, but understanding your own boundaries is essential. If you are working sixty-hour weeks because of a big push at work, perhaps you can do so for a month before hitting your personal limit. It is up to you to make changes before you reach your breaking point.

The final step involves balancing intense efforts with self-care. What hobbies or activities re-energize you after you feel drained? The answer is different for everyone. It may even be something physically grueling, like a challenging hike. The point isn't to stop all activity but to replenish yourself in a way that works for you.

## The Importance of Mindfulness

When I was a child, my mother's youngest sister, Cynthia, used to visit us for a few days at a time. One weekend morning, after waking up, I asked my mom, "What is Aunt Cynthia doing in the living room?" She had her eyes closed and was completely focused, as if she were in another world. It was the first time I saw someone meditating. Neither my mother nor I knew much about meditation. It wasn't mainstream at the time, but that didn't stop Aunt Cynthia. Little did I know her meditation practice would inspire me at a pivotal point in my life, many years later.

When the COVID-19 pandemic hit in 2020, I had been living life at a mile a minute. The pandemic provided me with an opportunity to slow down, be more present in the moment, and further recognize all the things in my life to be grateful for. I thought about Aunt Cynthia and decided to give meditation a shot.

I began meditating for five minutes each day, figuring it would be easy. After all, it was only five minutes. But about thirty seconds into my first session, my mind started to wander. Despite this, I managed to stay the course and made it through. I committed to try it for at least twenty-one consecutive days and was determined not to quit. Each day, it became easier to focus. Eventually, I meditated for ten minutes, and I still do so today.

Since taking up meditation almost five years ago, I've noticed a change in how I show up in the world. Before, I often felt overwhelmed with a million thoughts racing through my mind. Now, I feel less stressed and more present. When I encounter complex situations, I am also able to slow my mind down before acting.

Whether you've tried meditation before or you're skeptical like I was at first, I highly encourage you to give it a shot and be consistent every day. Start with five minutes, one minute, or even just thirty seconds. Dedicating time is the first step. After your first week, add another minute, then another after your second week, and so on. Give it a chance for at least three weeks and see if you notice a change. The journey of meditation can be deeply rewarding, and there are plenty of resources like books, podcasts, and classes to help guide you along the way.

James Lawrence, a world-record-holding triathlete, has a similar respect for mindfulness. On Jim Rome's podcast, *The Reinvention Project*, James expressed, "The mind is the most powerful asset we have. It can cripple you or it can advance you."[30] In other words, your mind is the driver of your journey, and meditation is an effective way to keep you focused.

## The Power of Friendship in Self-Care

Raising three young boys after my father's murder, my mother faced the difficult challenge of ensuring the well-being of her children. Dad's passing left a void that could never be filled, but Mom's determination and love never wavered. She took on responsibilities with a strength that seemed almost superhuman.

Her life became a testament to sacrifice. She often went without to make sure my brothers and I had what we needed. Working multiple jobs took a toll on her health, but I rarely heard her complain. She prioritized us above all else, ensuring we had opportunities for education and growth. As we grew older, the weight of our father's absence was always felt, but Mom's constant support provided us with a foundation of strength and resilience.

Twenty years after my father's death, my mom remarried, bringing a new chapter of love into her life with her second husband, Michael. However, Michael came with his own set of challenges. He had numerous physical problems and did not take good care of himself. The years that followed were filled with him having frequent hospitalizations, amputations, and strokes. Despite these challenges, Mom remained devoted to his care. When Michael died of complications from COVID-19 in May of 2020, it was another difficult loss for her, but also a release from a period of intense caregiving.

Not long after her second husband's passing, Mom once again assumed the role of caretaker, this time for her mother who was approaching her 100th birthday. Even with Mom's own health struggles, including multiple surgeries on her back and difficulty walking, she provided comfort to her mom during her final years.

After my grandmother passed away, Mom was finally able to focus more on herself. Despite her physical limitations, she finds joy and fulfillment in the relationships she has built over the years. Her friends and community provide a support system that enriches her life. These friendships, some of which have lasted for more than fifty years, are her lifeline. They are how she takes care of herself amidst the demands of caring for others.

When we talk, Mom often speaks about how fortunate she is to have such wonderful friends. For example, her sister, my Aunt Joyce, has been by my mom's side as a best friend throughout both of their lives. Mom's friends provide her with comfort and joy. Even when physical health is compromised, the emotional benefits of meaningful connections can greatly improve someone's life. Mom's story shows that nurturing strong relationships is an effective way to care for oneself, especially in challenging times.

## Help Others Take Care of Themselves

In discussing the various ways to be a mensch, you've probably noticed a common theme: being a mensch is not just about striving to be your best. It's also about supporting others in doing the same. This is especially true when it comes to finding balance and taking care of yourself. By taking care of your own well-being, you set an example and can better help others in their journey. In my experience, there are several ways you can do this.

First, model self-care and balance. As a manager or leader, you have a unique opportunity to impact your team members' ability to maintain balance by demonstrating it. Take your vacation days, and when you do, disconnect from work. Set personal boundaries and encourage others to do the same. Carve out time for exercise and mental breaks. If a team member has a personal emergency, do everything you can to cover their responsibilities and make it a priority to support whatever they are going through.

Second, engage with others by simply asking how they are. Be sincere. This small act can go a long way towards making others feel valued. Regular check-ins can help build a culture of openness and trust. For example, consider setting aside time during meetings to ask about team members' personal lives and stress levels. Showing that you care about them beyond work can strengthen your relationship and create a more supportive work environment.

Lastly, show up when others need help. Whether it's providing assistance on a project, offering a listening ear, or giving support during difficult times, your presence can make a significant difference. Consistently being there for others demonstrates reliability and fosters a sense of community. This kind of support can inspire others to adopt a similar approach, creating a ripple effect of kindness within your network.

Recently, a close friend wrote in her birthday card to me, "I am so happy for you and your family with the choices you've made to make family and balance a priority. It is such a gift you're giving yourself and those around you." To me, I'm simply staying focused and doing the work to be better every day, continuing to pull on that flywheel. Not only have I benefited, but also have those around me, who say they feel inspired to make changes in their own lives.

As you continue your journey to be the leader and person you want to become, ask those closest to you if they notice any changes. Sometimes, you can become so focused on the incremental movements of the flywheel that it's hard to see how much progress you've made. Take a step back and seek feedback from friends, family members, or colleagues who can offer an outside perspective. Their observations can provide valuable insights and encouragement, helping you recognize and celebrate your growth. Additionally, try keeping a journal to document your experiences and reflections. This practice can help you track your progress over time and serve as a reminder of how far you've come.

Recognizing the good in your life and maintaining balance will bring true happiness, which leads to the success you seek. As Louise Hay writes, "Rejoice in the abundance of being able to awaken each morning and experience a new day. Be glad to be alive, to be healthy, to have friends, to be creative, to be a living example of the joy of living."[31]

# Exercises

1) Transform Your Perspective.

Make a list of up to five things you "have to" do. Then, rewrite the list through the lens of things you "get to" do.

"I have to…"                "I get to…"

2) Accountability Partner.

Each month, choose one thing from the above list and pick an accountability partner to support you in following through. This could be someone from your network, a family member, or a friend.

3) Balance Your Efforts.

Reflect on the unseen hours you are investing along your journey and the optimal performance you are giving each day. Identify three activities that can help you counterbalance this effort. These could be hobbies, meditation practices, or anything else that replenishes you and enables you to continue giving your best.

## CHAPTER EIGHT

# A MENSCH SHOWS UP

The best way to find yourself is to lose yourself in the service of others.

Mahatma Ghandi

Growing up without my father was incredibly challenging and lonely. Some of my peers bullied me about his absence. One boy would regularly tease me, saying things like, "I've got something you'll never have," referring to having a father. Others mocked me for not wearing trendy clothes—clothes that my family couldn't afford on my mother's income, as she at one point worked four jobs to make ends meet.

As a young child who had lost so much, it was tempting to focus on what I didn't have. I didn't have a father. My family didn't have a lot of money. And, unfortunately, some of our extended family members failed to show up for us, even after they had said they would. Fortunately, somewhere along my journey, I learned to focus on what I did have rather than what I did not.

With this new mindset, I shifted my attention from the loss of my father to the presence of the many wonderful people I had in my life. There were five men in particular who truly showed up for me, serving as invaluable father figures and positive influences throughout my youth and long into adulthood. Each of them demonstrated what it means to be there for others and the powerful impact such actions can have on someone's life.

### Uncle Paul

Uncle Paul was married to my Aunt Joyce for many years before they divorced, yet he has always been there to support me, my mother, and my brothers. A couple of days after my father's death, he stepped in and hired a pharmacist for my dad's store because prescriptions needed to be filled for patients in need. Uncle Paul also played basketball games with me and my brothers in the driveway at his house and took us to Boston Celtics games. I've sought his advice countless times throughout the years and still do today. He tells great teaching stories and recently advised me, "You have to be resistant, consistent, and persistent." His wisdom and guidance have helped me reflect on and learn from the challenges in my life, ultimately making me stronger.

### David

My dad's cousin, David, was six years younger than my father, and the two of them shared a special bond that included ski trips and outings for ice cream. Though David had been a part of my life from day one, he became even more intentional in his support after Dad died. When I was eleven, he surprised me and my brothers by bringing

us to a World Series baseball game between the New York
Mets and the Boston Red Sox at Fenway Park. Years later,
he took me on visits to college campuses, encouraging
me to shoot for the stars. We still connect almost every
day, and he often shares stories about my dad and offers
encouraging words for my future.

*Tony*

My mother dated Tony from the time I was ten until my
early twenties. Tony was a hardworking mason with a thick
Italian accent and a habit of bringing home more pizza than
we could ever eat. He was the first to teach me how to drive
and helped me move into college. While he could never
replace my dad and never tried to, he was there for many
of the things I know my dad would have been there for.
He showed up genuinely and kindly, with no awkwardness
or resentment, even during the years when I was lashing
out. "You have to suffer to enjoy," he told my mom once.
That was Tony. His positive attitude made it easy for me
to like and respect him.

*Joel*

While I grew up on the East Coast, my cousin Joel lived
across the country in California, so I did not see him very
much. However, from the time I moved to California in
2002 until he died of cancer in 2015, he was a significant
father figure in my life. My kids called him and his wife,
Ann, "Nana and Papa." Joel was a very successful business-

man and mentored me throughout most of my professional career. He taught me many lessons that have transcended into all areas of my life. I frequently sought his advice on specific challenges, drawing on his extensive experience from traveling around the world for business.

Something that I'll never forget is how he'd swing by our house on his way home from business trips to drop off souvenirs for Alex and Marina. He'd loosen his tie, get down on the floor, and announce, "I'm going to give you a rinky dink!" before scooping them up by their legs and tickling their stomachs while they giggled uncontrollably. These moments taught me the importance of balancing work with quality family time.

*Poppi*

I called my mother's father Poppi. Though he and my grandmother weren't wealthy in a financial sense, they were rich with love and gave me and my brothers as much as they could. Poppi was a sportswriter and overall sports fanatic—a great point of connection between us—and he always found new ways to teach life lessons through sports. One time, he took me to a baseball card show where we met Hall of Fame pitcher Warren Spahn. During my introduction to Mr. Spahn, Poppi taught me the importance of a firm handshake and looking someone in the eye. He had a knack for turning simple moments into valuable teaching lessons.

My life would not have been the same without these five mensches. While I didn't choose to grow up without a father, each of them chose to walk alongside me on my journey. All I had to do was welcome their guidance and love. This experience taught me an early lesson in the importance of leaning on others for support. More significantly, these men encouraged me not to let adversity stop me from living my best life. They showed me that there was much more in store for me beyond the pain I had experienced—as long as I stayed on the path of resilience. I never could've imagined how much these men would shape my life, but they gave me the strength to keep going, even when things were tough. Their support and belief in me showed me that no matter how hard life gets, there's always a way forward.

## The Little Things

At Poppi's funeral in 2014, as I stood at the podium delivering my eulogy, I glanced up and saw one of my colleagues seated in the audience with his wife, Suzeanne. It was Mark, the coworker I introduced in Chapter 4, who had given me invaluable feedback that helped me become a better teammate and leader. I was deeply moved and surprised to see them there, especially considering they had three young kids, demanding jobs, and lived far away. I'm sure they had a hundred other things they could have done that day, but they chose to show up for me and my family. It may have seemed like a small gesture to them, but it meant a lot to me.

Sometimes, a seemingly small action can make a big difference in someone else's life. This is something I try to do whenever I can as a leader. Years ago, when I was the vice president of a global team of about sixty people, before everyone left the office for our annual two-week winter shutdown, I handwrote a personalized note to each of them. These notes meant a great deal, as most had not received such acknowledgment from senior leaders in their careers. I always made sure to carve out the time to make this small gesture because I knew how impactful it would be.

Showing up for others doesn't always require an excessive amount of time or resources. It is simply about letting them know that someone cares about them. Small things, like sending a thoughtful message, lending a listening ear, or offering help during tough times, can build stronger connections and create a supportive environment. As a leader, demonstrating this level of care can inspire others to do the same, creating a culture of kindness and support.

## Stand Up for Others

Sometimes, showing up for others means being there for them even when they're not in the room. After several years of working with a leader I admired, he moved on to a new chapter in his career. But his imprint on our company remained. Two years after his departure, we had many new team members, all of whom had heard about everything he had done for our highly successful company. So, I wasn't surprised when, while out to lunch with several others, the topic of his leadership came up. What did surprise me, though, was what one of my colleagues had to say when the conversation turned to an issue we had been dealing with.

He said, "It's clear that [former leader] is at fault for all of this. Was anyone else responsible for this mess we're in, or was it just him?" Nobody corrected his outrageous statement. Everyone remained silent.

I'll admit that I was a little reluctant to speak up at that moment and say what was clearly an unpopular truth. It would have been much easier to keep quiet and focus on my lunch. But I spoke up. "I'm not sure what 'mess' you're referring to or why you think he has anything to do with it. I worked with him for many years, so perhaps I can clear up any confusion." Following an awkward discussion, his name was fully cleared of the false accusation.

What bothered me most about this interaction—aside from the comment—was that some others at that table knew the facts, yet I was the only one who spoke up. I can only assume that they stayed silent because they saw protecting their former colleague's legacy and making sure the truth was known as a low priority. It was easier to allow the person who wasn't in the room to get run over by the proverbial bus. I couldn't help but wonder whether someone, someday, would care enough to speak up in my defense when it matters.

## Keep Your Commitments

I previously shared the story of my contact who agreed to have an introductory call with a former colleague but didn't follow through and eventually told me he was just too busy. This example highlighted the importance of being honest about your limitations.

I bring it up again to reiterate the importance of following through on your commitments.

This is a standard I have set for myself and is included in my personal identity statement. However, my experience has been that many people do not follow through on what they say they will do. Even those who seem reliable can sometimes fall short. As was the case with my former colleague who never met with my contact, people sometimes make commitments they cannot logistically keep, and that's okay. People make mistakes. But if you realize you cannot keep a promise, admit it, and seek a way to make amends.

## How Leaders and Organizations Show Up

How you show up as a leader at work is vital. Especially if you are a people manager, there are numerous ways to show up for your team. The very best organizations are recognized for how they support their employees. I have been fortunate to be on the receiving and giving ends of such support in my professional career.

The birth of our second child, Marina, in 2007 was a joyous yet stressful time for our family. I was working as a product manager for a medical device company and navigating a challenging new product launch amid mounting uncertainty over the company's future. My department was facing issues outside of our control, and instead of searching for solutions, it seemed as though different teams had begun to play the blame game, pointing fingers at others to keep the heat off themselves. I had recently completed my MBA program, and Mindy and I had our hands full at home with our energetic two-year-old, Alex. Into this whirlwind, Marina was born ten days earlier than we expected.

Thankfully, our growing family didn't have to juggle everything alone. Two close friends who had offered to help when Mindy went into labor kept their promise and showed up at the hospital. They brought Alex home with them and dropped him off at our house the next day.

Twenty-four hours later, in a joyful yet sleep-deprived haze and feeling anxious about taking a few weeks off from work, I walked to our mailbox where I found an envelope from my department leaders at work. Inside was a letter that read:

> Mindy and Todd,
> We want to wish you congratulations on the birth of your daughter! As a gift to your family, we would like to offer you lunch and dinner service for the week from Restaurants on the Run. For your convenience, an account has already been set up for you under Todd's name. Wishing you and your family all the best.

I can't tell you how much this gift meant to us. Even amid a very challenging workplace environment, my managers chose to support me and did so in an incredibly thoughtful way. What a mensch-like move! More than seventeen years later, I'm still grateful and have taken every opportunity to pay their kindness forward. I've also made sure to empower other leaders to go above and beyond to make their team members feel valued and appreciated.

In addition to supporting employees in their personal lives, there are many ways to help them professionally. Formal recognition such as celebrating employee milestones and acknowledging significant contributions are powerful ways to show up for your teammates. The ways in which you interact with your colleagues can also go a long way. Actively listening to them during conversations makes them feel valued. Promoting a healthy work-life balance by setting an example and encouraging that of others can impact the culture of an entire organization.

If you are a team leader, you can provide team members with opportunities for professional development, such as encouraging them to take courses or attend conferences that will expand their knowledge and network. Take the time to understand what is most important to each of them and strive to provide what they need to be successful. However you choose to show up for and support others, I've found that sincerity is always key.

## Just Roll Up Your Sleeves

In the summer of 2023, Mindy, Alex, and I traveled to Northern California to move Alex into his new place for his first year of college. He would be living in a house with a few other students, and we had heard it needed some work, so I brought some tools just in case. However, nothing could have prepared us for what we walked into.

We flew up five days before his classes began, giving us plenty of time to get him settled in. Before heading to the house, we stopped at the property management company to pick up a set of keys. When we arrived at the house, it didn't look too bad from the outside. However, as we opened the door, our stomachs sank.

The house was a disaster. The previous tenants had left dirty clothes on the floor, empty beer bottles were everywhere, broken glass was in the couch, and a terrible smell permeated the entire place. We learned that for ten years, the lease had been handed over from tenant to tenant with no real move-in or move-out cleaning.

As Mindy and I saw the disappointment and concern on Alex's face, we assured him that it was going to be okay. We had plenty of time to roll up our sleeves and improve the condition of the house. Fortunately, we had already arranged for professional cleaners to help the following morning. They contacted me shortly after we arrived at the house, asking if they could come by that afternoon to check out the job. Of course, I said "yes," but I worried that once they saw the place, they might back out. Thankfully, they were reliable and committed to coming back in the morning.

That afternoon, Mindy, Alex, and I removed everything from the house. And I mean everything—dishes, clothing, trash, the furniture, and even old cleaning supplies that appeared to have never been used. We made a giant pile in the yard, and by the end of the night, we had an empty house. Although it was still filthy, it gave us a blank slate to work with.

After the cleaners arrived the following morning, I went to Home Depot to pick up some paint and various renovation supplies. Over the next four days, we transformed the house and added some basic furniture and kitchen items. When Alex's housemates arrived, one of them said to Mindy and me, "We're so glad you're here and that you did all of this." They were thrilled to have a clean and comfortable home.

The night before school started, the house was ready for Alex to sleep there for the first time. When most parents take their child to college, they spend a couple of hours settling them into a clean dorm room and then head back home. In our case, we spent four days with Alex. We shared meals, got to know his housemates, and had good conversations while scrubbing, painting, and furnishing the house. Once it was finally time for us to go, we were ready to say goodbye (at least as ready as a parent ever feels). As I hugged him, I realized how fortunate Mindy and I had been to spend the past four days together and set our child up for success in the next chapter of his life.

This experience made me reflect on how we show up for those we care about. When someone is in need, the first thing we tend to do is ask how we can help. This is important because to effectively show up for others, you must first know how you can support them. Instead of just asking "How can I help?" which can sometimes feel empty, offering specific suggestions for what you might be able to do is more practical. For example, questions like: Can I bring dinner to you and your family tomorrow night? How about I pick your kids up from school and bring them home this afternoon? Sometimes, you already know what needs to be done, and in those instances, a mensch will just do it.

## Showing Up When Asked

In the high-stakes environment of the operating room, where every second counts, even the most experienced surgeons can face unexpected challenges. One day, while representing my company as a product manager, I was working with a surgeon who found himself in such a situation. Despite his expertise, he couldn't reach a critical part of a patient's brain with the catheters that he inserted into her. Time was running out, and the methods he tried weren't working.

The surgeon asked his team for ideas, but no one had a solution that worked. Then he turned to me. Having traveled extensively and observed surgeons from around the world, I had seen many different techniques. A situation in Germany came to mind, where a doctor faced a similar problem and used a unique method to solve it.

I shared what the surgeon did in Germany. This is one of the great benefits of working with different people: everyone has unique experiences and insights that can be helpful. He decided to try the technique I described. As he followed the method, everyone in the room watched the monitor closely to track the catheter's location. To everyone's relief, it worked.

Afterwards, the surgeon turned around and thanked me for speaking up and helping. By simply sharing an observation from my travels, I had played a part in saving a life. In that moment, I felt a deep sense of fulfillment. It was a powerful reminder of the value of shared knowledge and the importance of being open to learning from others.

Listening and learning, even when the information doesn't seem immediately relevant, can be incredibly important later. You never know how valuable what you are learning now can be in the future. Had I not paid attention to what the surgeon was doing in Germany years earlier, I wouldn't have gained the knowledge that helped someone else in this critical moment. This principle applies not just to surgeons, but to everyone: always be learning, because what you learn today might come in handy and possibly even save a life someday.

## How It Feels to Show Up for Others

Jeremy was a criminal defense attorney with a quick wit, great personality, and commanding presence. He was deeply involved in the community, but his greatest passion was his family. Jeremy and his wife, Debra, had three children who, in 2020, were 17, 15, and 11 years old. Mindy and I became friends with them when their middle son and Alex were in the same preschool class. Whenever our families got together, we chatted about sports, travel, business, and our families.

On Monday night, November 16, 2020, just a day after our families spent the afternoon at an outdoor park together, Jeremy collapsed and died after exercising. I was shocked when we heard about the tragedy the following day. My thoughts immediately went to the loss of my own father, the impact it had on my entire life, and what Debra and her children must have been going through. Despite the shock and the challenging circumstances, we wanted to provide our support and went directly to their house. Jeremy and Debra were very giving members of our community, so it was no surprise that many people were already there when we arrived.

When I saw Debra, I hugged her and told her that my family would be there for whatever her family needed. I assumed they heard this from many others, but as my mom told me from her experience after the tragic death of my father, actions speak louder than words. I knew how important it would be—especially in the coming months—for people to just show up for them, without being asked. And that is exactly what my family did and continues to do. Whether it's bringing a grocery bag filled with fresh food or fixing things around the house, the point is to be present, so they know we are there for them. For the children specifically, I also thought it might be helpful for them to see an example of someone who faced similar adversity and has gone on to live a fulfilled life.

Debra and her three kids have expressed how thankful they are for everything we have done and continue to do for them. But what I've told her many times is how good it feels to make a positive difference in their lives. Of course, being a mensch is not about what you gain from helping others. A mensch shows up for others without expecting anything in return. However, when you show up for others repeatedly, you will likely gain something. *When you lift others, they will also lift you up.*

In one of my mother's letters to me and my brothers back in 1986, she wrote about how small the world is and emphasized the importance of building a positive reputation. She encouraged us to respect ourselves in a way that would result in others respecting us as well. Over the years, I've expanded on Mom's guidance by adding the importance of showing up for others and following through on my commitments. Holding myself to this standard has earned me a reputation as someone others can rely on.

In essence, part of being a mensch means showing up for others, standing up for them, and building strong, meaningful relationships through your actions. By consistently demonstrating integrity, empathy, and support, you create a foundation of trust that strengthens both your personal and professional connections. These qualities and the meaningful relationships they foster are essential aspects of what it truly means to be a mensch.

# Exercises

1) Identify Someone in Need.

Who in your life might be in need of someone to show up for them? Consider their circumstances and think of ways you can offer support without even having to ask.

2) Daily Compliments Challenge.

Commit to giving unsolicited, genuine compliments to at least three people per day for a week. Note any changes in your relationships and how the act of giving compliments affects your own mood and outlook.

3) Acts of Kindness Journal.

For one week, record daily acts of kindness—both those you receive and those you offer—regardless of how small. Reflect on how these acts affected you and the recipients and consider how you can incorporate such gestures into your life more regularly.

## CHAPTER NINE

# A MENSCH SUCCEEDS
# WITH OTHERS

Alone we can do so little; together we can do so much.

Helen Keller

Picture yourself standing at the base of a mountain. Not your local hiking trail, but a real mountain with jagged, snow-covered rock faces and a summit shrouded in its own weather system. As you stand there, loaded down with gear and supplies, you try to muster the strength and confidence to start the climb—a grueling, weeks-long excursion that you've been training to tackle for years.

Now, imagine you're not alone. Surrounding you is a group of equally prepared climbers, each ready to conquer the mountain. They also have the necessary gear, supplies, and training. The time has come for you to begin. Do you set off by yourself, or do you join the group?

Climbing with others offers numerous benefits. You'll have motivation, support when you stumble, and someone to help lighten your load when you are tired. Everyone also brings various skills—one might build a strong shelter, another might have excellent navigation skills, and someone else might be medically trained.

Life is no different. Having the support of others makes achieving your goals more attainable. Whether you're climbing a mountain, launching a new product, or battling an illness, you're almost always better off making your journey with others.

## Cultivating Your Fairy Ring

When Mindy and I lived in Boston, we took a week-long trip to the San Francisco Bay Area. During our stay, we decided to visit Muir Woods National Monument. This forest, filled with towering redwood trees that are hundreds of years old, was awe-inspiring.

One fascinating fact about redwood trees is how they grow to be hundreds of feet tall. Some of them sprout in circles called "fairy rings," with their roots intertwined to provide mutual support. This network of roots is crucial for their survival and growth. Just as the trees rely on each other to withstand storms and reach great heights, people also need a network of supportive relationships to help navigate challenges and achieve their goals.

Developing your own fairy ring of supportive relationships is key. By cultivating these relationships, those who care about your success will be there to support you when needed. This mutual investment makes you stronger and more likely to achieve your goals than if you were to travel alone.

A mensch supports others by standing up for them and lending their strength when needed. When they succeed, everyone shares in the joy of that success. Jim Collins writes in *Good to Great*, "Those who build great companies understand that the ultimate throttle on growth for any great company is not markets, or technology, or competition, or products. It is one thing above all others: the ability to get and keep enough of the right people."[32] For people to stay with an organization, they need to feel valued and supported. This is why one of the greatest things a leader can do is build a sense of shared purpose and a culture of collaboration and trust within their team.

## Building Owners in Your Success

Just as a mensch supports others, building a network of people who are invested in your success is crucial for personal and professional growth. These are individuals who support you and genuinely want to see you succeed. But how do you go about building this network? One effective way is by asking others for their help. I once worked with two people, Ryan and David, who were in similar roles. Both had strong backgrounds and potential for success. Ryan chose to work independently and stayed at his desk, while David engaged with colleagues and sought their advice and support. Unsurprisingly, David performed better and advanced faster. Most people find it rewarding to help others. When David asked his team members for advice, they saw it as an opportunity to contribute, which they found fulfilling.

There are also many other ways to build owners in your success. For example, throughout my career, I've made it a point to personally welcome my new colleagues, regardless of whether we were in the same department. Despite the busyness of corporate life, taking just thirty seconds to offer a warm welcome and your support can make a significant difference. A quick email to make someone feel welcome is sometimes all it takes.

Now, think about how many of these people could become owners in your success. You'd be surprised at how many might support you and your team without you even knowing it. It's a testament to how a small act of kindness can have a long-lasting impact.

## Treat Others How *They* Want to Be Treated

Just as building a supportive network is essential for success, knowing others' preferences is critical for positive relationships. People often follow the "Golden Rule": treat others as you want to be treated. However, this can be problematic if others' preferences differ from your own. That's why many experts advocate for the "Platinum Rule": treat others as *they* want to be treated.

One day, my colleague Aaron vented his frustration to me about another coworker. He had emailed her a question and sent two follow-up emails, all of which went unanswered. "Try calling her or swinging by her office," I suggested. "That's how she prefers to communicate." Aaron was baffled; he wouldn't like it if someone popped into his office in the middle of the day. However, he gave it a try, and they resolved the issue. Understanding and respecting his colleague's communication preferences made all the difference.

In the workplace, I've found the best way to apply the Platinum Rule is by offering others support rather than demanding theirs. In 2010, as a new senior product manager, I spent half of my first six months traveling across the United States to work with our local sales representatives. When they asked about my goals,

I explained that I wanted to understand their needs so I could focus on projects that would make the biggest impact for them and our customers.

These travels also helped me build strong relationships. In my experience, one of the best ways to build relationships in the workplace is to work alongside colleagues. During my trips, I rode with them on long drives from state to state, giving us plenty of time to talk. I learned a lot from these conversations and appreciated the opportunity for them to learn more about me, both personally and professionally. We also shared many laughs. During one trip, my colleague and I stopped for gas in the middle of Ohio. While he filled the tank, I went into the convenience store and walked out with two bottles of water, granola bars, and a New England Patriots windbreaker jacket. Finding the jacket of my favorite football team in such an unexpected place felt like fate, so I decided to buy it. My colleague thought this was hilarious, and now, more than fourteen years later, every time I wear it, I think of him and the great time we had on that trip.

While my travels cultivated strong bonds and valuable insights, not all interactions in the workplace were this positive. During these trips, I discovered that one of my colleagues back at the office was intentionally withholding information from me. Though I never fully understood her motives, I suspected they were tied to events before my arrival at the company.

Once I was aware of her actions, I decided to keep my head high, my eyes wide open, and always be respectful. I was careful not to stoop to her level of behavior. I've seen too many people do this, and it only drags everyone down. Instead, I held firm to my mensch mindset and did my best to treat others how they wanted to be treated.

## The Power of Team Building

One September, my team of fifty and I took a one-day adventure to Catalina Island, a short boat ride from the Southern California coast. We had planned the outing two months earlier, right after surpassing our corporate objectives, and everyone was looking forward to this special day. Recognizing the value of stepping away from the office to take a break and get to know each other better, we had offsite team-building days a few times each year.

Upon our arrival on the island, we set up a basecamp with themed drinks, food, and music for everyone to enjoy. In the middle of the day, there were various activities to choose from, including zip lining, a Jeep tour, kayaking, parasailing, and exploring the town. The primary goal was for everyone to have fun and build relationships with each other. Also, all of these activities encouraged people to try something new.

One team member, who had always wanted to parasail but was afraid to try it alone, confronted her fears with a colleague by her side and had a fantastic time. This is what individuals do for each other: they help each other overcome obstacles that are harder to face alone, lend a helping hand, and lead the way for others to follow.

Back at the office, a team member was nervous about presenting to the entire team. His colleagues helped him prepare his slides and practice several times. When the time came for his presentation, he was still nervous, but his preparation paid off. He delivered a fantastic presentation to thirty colleagues. The look on his face was priceless when everyone clapped and congratulated him. It wasn't just his success; everyone who helped him prepare felt a shared sense of accomplishment. They were all owners in his success.

Challenging yourself not only strengthens individual skills but also fosters strong relationships. These relationships then carry forward to other projects, enabling teammates to support each other throughout their shared work journey. When individuals take on challenges together, they develop a stronger connection. This leads to more effective collaboration, innovative problem-solving, and a better team dynamic. As team members continue to support each other, they also create an environment where everyone feels valued and motivated.

Many organizations silo their people, and some individuals silo themselves, treating colleagues as competitors. Great organizations and leaders, however, create environments where people thrive by supporting each other and succeeding together. Leaders set an example by venturing outside their comfort zone and being vulnerable with their teams. This approach fosters a culture of openness, where team members feel empowered to take risks and support each other.

For example, when I wanted to learn more about venture capital, I signed up for a week-long course on it. I was open and honest about my knowledge gap, asking several of my team members for their advice while preparing for the course. By showing this vulnerability, I signaled to my team that it was safe for them to step outside their comfort zones as well. As a result, we saw increased collaboration and a greater willingness to tackle new challenges together.

Organizing team building days can be challenging, especially when there's always work to be done. However, just as personal balance is a key to individual success, organizational balance is also important. Team building activities can offer the perfect opportunity to help your team recharge and connect.

When organizing an upcoming offsite for my team several years ago, six members volunteered to assist with the planning. Our objectives were to ensure that everyone learned, strengthened relationships, and had a good time. Shortly after initiating the planning, the team created a brand for the event, naming it "C3"—Communicate, Collaborate, and Connect.

Alongside the C3 branding, they chose a "Rocky" theme, inspired by the iconic movie character and the coincidental name of our venue, the Balboa Hotel. They also transformed the conference room into a boxing-themed environment. A life-size cardboard cutout of Rocky stood at the front, boxing gloves served as table centerpieces, and various props were scattered throughout the room. The atmosphere was topped off with songs from the Rocky soundtrack playing during the meeting.

The first group activity involved creating a team culture statement. During interviews with new associates, candidates often asked about our department's culture. However, without a consistent statement, our descriptions varied. We decided it was best to develop a unified one together, so we worked through the session to craft a statement that reflected our team's values. To keep it visible when we returned to the office, we created displays for everyone's workspace and included it in the opening slides of our monthly department meetings.

The second activity focused on training the team on the recently defined company core values. To introduce them, we split into groups and lined up facing a Rocky punching bag at the back of the conference room. When the facilitator described an action representing one of the core values, the teams that correctly identified the value first took a step toward the punching bag. For instance, if "giving a team member the opportunity to take ownership of a particular project" was read, the core value would be empowerment. The team that reached the punching bag first won.

The third activity was also highly impactful. Everyone had completed the DiSC personal assessment tool, which helps improve teamwork, communication, and productivity in the workplace.[33] The assessment determines how your work style aligns with these traits and how to best collaborate with your colleagues.

A DiSC expert facilitated the session to make sure we got the most out of it. She walked us through our results and showed how different styles can either complement each other or lead to misunderstandings. Through interactive exercises and discussions, we learned how to adjust our communication style to better match our colleagues' preferences. This helped us apply the Platinum Rule in our interactions and gain a deeper understanding of each other.

## Reflecting on Team Building Success

These activities didn't just help our team bond—they also gave us valuable tools to help us work better together. By getting out of the office and engaging in fun activities, we were able to strengthen our relationships and improve our collaborative efforts. This balance of work and play is essential for maintaining a healthy and productive team environment.

As we wrapped up day one of our offsite meeting, I took a moment to thank everyone for their active participation and the planners of the event. To my surprise, as I finished my remarks, the team presented me with a framed photo featuring Rocky Balboa's quote: "Going in one more round when you don't think you can. That's what makes all the difference in your life." Five of my team members shared some kind words about my leadership, moving me to tears. Seeing this, several team members were also visibly touched.

Crying in the workplace is uncommon, yet it's a natural expression of our emotions. Unfortunately, society often perceives such displays as a sign of weakness. I believe that vulnerability requires courage and is key to being authentic. Everyone faces challenges, struggles, and emotions. By opening up and sharing your own, you create an environment that encourages others to do the same.

When my team saw me cry in the front of the room, they knew I was being genuine. I was deeply moved by their generosity and expressed my appreciation for their kind gift, their words, our special day, and their trust in me as their leader. For the first time, I shared with them the story of my father's murder and explained why Rocky means so much to me. Watching the Rocky movies as a child, quotes like "Going in one more round when you don't think you can" symbolized the resilience I was striving for and helped me through some very challenging times.

As I spoke, the room was silent. Before that day, almost none of them knew about the tragedy I faced and what I had overcome. I had been reluctant to share my story because I didn't want them to feel sorry for me. However, that's not what happened. They were inspired by what I shared and got to know much more about me as a person.

In the weeks that followed, dozens of team members thanked me for being so open with them. There wasn't any sympathy—just gratitude. Many of them also shared some of their most challenging times with me. By sharing my story, I helped them feel comfortable sharing theirs.

A few weeks after the event, I was surprised to receive a letter and a vinyl record of the Rocky soundtrack from one of my team members and his wife. The letter read:

Dear Todd,

We, as humans, never really know what someone else has had to endure in their lifetime albeit short or long. That being said, Bob shared with me how the movie *Rocky* helped you personally cope with your family's very tragic loss. "Rocky = Gonna Fly Now" has helped a lot of us along the way of life! Bob and I share a love for collecting vintage albums, especially from all the cool bands he has seen from his concert-going days. Ironically, we found this original motion picture score album by Bill Conti. Long story short...we thought of you. I played it, and it sounds great. We hope you enjoy it and think of us. Todd—Here's to going the distance!

Fondly, Donna and Bob

Receiving this letter and thoughtful gift underscored how sharing my story created a ripple effect, extending beyond just the people in the room. It sparked conversations that touched others. Donna only heard about my story from Bob, yet she was moved to reach out and express her support. This demonstrates how being vulnerable can create a broader impact.

As Brené Brown writes in *The Power of Vulnerability*, "When we dare to drop the armor that protects us from feeling vulnerable, we open ourselves to the experiences that bring purpose and meaning to our lives."[34] We all shared a heartfelt, honest experience that day, which really brought us together as a team.

In his book, *Start With Why*, Simon Sinek explains how world-renowned companies like Apple don't just sell products—they make people feel connected to their brand. Sinek calls this strategy "The Golden Circle of Why, How, and What." While many businesses focus on what they do or how they do it, the most successful ones start with why they do it. That's what really resonates with customers. This approach isn't just for companies; it's also a powerful tool for leaders. If you want to inspire your team, you can tell them what to do or how to do it. But to truly motivate them, they need to understand and believe in the mission—the why behind it all.

I realized after our team's offsite that sharing my personal story was powerful because it revealed my why. Before that day, my team knew me mostly as Todd Zive, a senior executive in the medical technology industry who was committed to helping them succeed. By understanding my *why*, my team was further compelled to rally around our company's mission and objectives. If you want to be a leader who motivates others, or if you simply want to inspire those around you, I strongly recommend articulating and demonstrating your why.

Just like the redwood tree fairy rings, a cohesive team is much stronger than any individual. As I developed my mensch mindset, I learned the importance of embracing others, having them join me along my journey, and recognizing the value of doing the same for them. Instead of focusing solely on your own achievements and going at it alone, focus on raising the performance of those around you, and trust that the results will take care of themselves.

# Exercises

1) Identify a Challenge or Area for Support.

   What is an area or a challenge in your life where you might be resisting the support of others, or where you could benefit from embracing the support of others?

2) Seek Willing Partners.

   From your answer to number one above, who in your life might be willing to join you on this part of your journey?

3) Cultivate Vulnerability.

What are some ways you can be more vulnerable with others, at work or in your personal life?

4) Extend Support to Others.

Reach out to three people in your network and ask how you can support them at this current stage in their journey. Make specific commitments to help them and follow through on each one.

# CHAPTER TEN

# A MENSCH TRUSTS THE JOURNEY

The only impossible journey is the one you never begin.

Tony Robbins

Of all the countries I've visited around the world, Hawaii is one of my favorite places. A few years ago, during a family vacation there, Mindy, Alex, Marina, and I decided to explore the famous Road to Hana, a scenic and winding route along the north side of the island that ends in the small town of Hana. The road is so tight and winding that, for many stretches, you can't travel faster than five miles per hour.

We crossed single-lane bridges and passed several waterfalls along the drive. Our guidebook suggested a hike to a beautiful waterfall hidden in the forest. The directions advised us to pull over after mile marker thirteen, park on the side of the road, and take a short hike. After finding just enough room to park right up against the trees, we set off on the trail.

We entered through a small opening in the trees that we would not have noticed without the guidebook's specific directions. The rugged path led us to a stream, likely runoff from a larger waterfall. Even though we couldn't hear it, we saw the slow current making its way through the boulders, rocks, and sticks at our feet. Walking through the water seemed like the only way forward, so Marina and I took the lead while Alex and Mindy followed closely behind.

After about forty-five minutes, we heard rushing water and noticed that the stream's current was picking up speed. As we continued to traverse the boulders, the sound of water grew louder with every step. After turning a corner, we were met with an enormous, picturesque waterfall that was about eighty feet high—simply magical. We were all blown away.

I've seen many amazing sights across the thirty-five countries I've visited, but none came close to this. As we splashed around, Alex said, "Dad, you see…we had to focus on every step at our feet without worrying about the waterfall ahead. If we looked up or moved too quickly, we might have fallen or gotten off track and not made it." He was absolutely right. If you're too fixated on your destination, you could lose sight of the steps you need to take to get there or, even worse, miss the special detours that life presents along the way.

## Embracing Flexibility Over Rigid Planning

In the corporate world, almost everything operates according to a plan. Financial targets are set annually, strategic decisions are aligned with these targets, and resources are allocated to support these decisions. It's like an intricate dance, with everything finding its place in the choreography. However, what I've learned throughout my journey is that things don't always go according to plan in business or in life.

As I navigated my own career changes in recent years, I found the messages of author Joanne Lipman particularly insightful. She notes that typical advice from personal development books and business leaders often suggests developing a concrete plan and meticulously executing it. However, after interviewing numerous professionals who made complex career and life changes, Lipman observes, "For many of those I interviewed, it was the opposite process—the actions they took led them to discover the goal, not the other way around."[35]

If you've ever interviewed for a corporate job, you've probably been asked the cliché question, "Where do you see yourself in ten years?" Many professionals, especially those early in their careers, welcome this question because they have a clear-cut answer. They have a specific goal and a precise plan for achieving it. However, this interview question doesn't truly capture a person's potential or adaptability.

Having a long-term goal in mind—a sense of direction—is helpful. But when life throws a twist into your path or your goals evolve, it's important to be flexible. As a leader, I'm less concerned with where someone plans to be in ten years, knowing that they'll probably end up somewhere different than they expect. I'm more interested in what they hope to experience along their journey and how prepared they are to handle any surprises that come their way.

## The Journey Is Unexpected

Marina has always marched to the beat of her own drum. While many teenage girls are making TikToks, Marina plays Led Zeppelin and Pink Floyd on her electric guitar, dances ballet, and creates unique art pieces.

During the COVID-19 pandemic, when she was in eighth grade, we heard good things about a local public art high school that was about twenty minutes from our house. Marina was interested in applying, so we submitted an application with the hope that she would start there in ninth grade. The school, in high demand, used a lottery system for admission. Despite completing the required art pieces to qualify for the lottery, Marina's draw number placed her in the fifty-fourth position on the waitlist, with only seven available spots. It was clear she would not be attending.

While we were disappointed, Marina quickly shifted her focus towards making the most out of attending her local public high school. In ninth grade, she joined the school's Dance Company, connecting with other talented artists who choreographed dances and produced shows throughout the year. She also seized the opportunity to perform the national anthem on her electric guitar for the baseball team's special games and tournaments. These opportunities might not have been available to her at the art school, where competition for such activities would have been much more intense.

Although Marina was disappointed about not being able to attend the art school, she has enjoyed her high school experience. The saying "things happen for a reason" rings true, but I would expand it to "things happen and sometimes don't happen for a reason." Being denied a particular path can lead to unexpected opportunities down another, just like it did for Marina.

In the winter of 2022, with Marina flourishing in high school and Alex preparing for college, everything seemed to be going smoothly for our family. But life often surprises us. One early December day, Mindy suddenly lost most of her hearing in her right ear, leading to an MRI that revealed a brain tumor. However, the tumor was completely unrelated to her hearing loss, making its discovery a blessing that may have saved her life.

Fortunately, I had worked with many doctors from around the world for the past twenty-five years, so I reached out to two of them for referrals to neurosurgeons. They both spoke very highly about Dr. Steven Giannotta at USC Keck Hospital in Los Angeles, so we made an appointment with him right away.

Dr. Giannotta, his physician assistant Dawn Fishback, and their entire team were amazing. They explained the need for brain surgery to remove the tumor and what to expect throughout the process. We scheduled the surgery for a week after Mindy's fiftieth birthday party in late April, allowing enough time for her to recover and feel well enough to attend Alex's high school graduation ceremony in June.

Embracing positive thinking, we envisioned the tumor disappearing and Mindy making a full recovery. Her birthday party was great, with everyone focused on celebrating Mindy and enjoying friends and family. The morning of the surgery, we saw the following handwritten message just outside the operating room:

"We want you to win. The entire universe is behind you. The only thing in your way is you. Think positive thoughts.

See yourself in possession of the life you dream of living. You become what you think about!"

This message was exactly what we needed to see at that moment and was consistent with what we had been visualizing.

The surgery lasted longer than expected, but it went well. Dr. Giannotta explained that the tumor was aggressive, making its discovery even more of a blessing. Four days later, Mindy was discharged from the hospital after receiving excellent care. She faced some minor challenges during her recovery, but her excellent health, our positive mindset, and the support of our community made a significant difference. Our friends organized a meal train, bringing dinner to our house every night for six weeks. Six months later, her follow-up MRI showed that the tumor was gone. Dr. Giannotta encouraged us to forget about the tumor and live our lives, and that he would see us again in a year for her next scan.

Reflecting on this experience, I realized how fortunate we were to have Dr. Giannotta as our neurosurgeon and to be surrounded by such a strong support system. My career had connected me to top neurosurgeons, and our community rallied around us when we needed them most. This journey taught us the power of positivity, the importance of strong connections, and the value of leaning on those around us when life takes unexpected turns.

## The Unstoppable Spirit

In life, it's crucial to remember that the path to success is often winding and filled with setbacks. Having faith in your journey, especially when things don't go as planned, is essential. A great example of this is the story of my son's friend and high school classmate, Paolo, and his ambitious goal of running one hundred continuous miles.

Paolo set this goal when he was only fifteen years old and immediately began training. As an upperclassman in high school, he was ready to achieve it. His plan was to start early in the morning, aiming to complete the one hundred-mile journey within twenty-four hours. The chosen route was the Back Bay Loop, a ten-mile circuit that he planned to complete ten times.

To support Paolo, his close friends from school, including Alex, set up an aid station every ten miles. This provided Paolo with the necessary rest, nutrition, and resources to keep going. They also took turns either riding a bike alongside him or running with him, so he never felt alone. Paolo's family played a significant role in his journey as well. They offered constant support, ensuring he had everything he needed.

In the early spring of 2023, Paolo's determination was unwavering as he started his run. After sixteen hours, he had covered an impressive sixty miles. However, his body could no longer endure the strain, forcing him to stop. Despite the disappointment, Paolo's spirit remained unbroken. Shortly after, he faced another challenge when he tore his ACL (anterior cruciate ligament), requiring surgery followed by several months of physical therapy.

Throughout this challenging time, Paolo's friends and family continued to offer their support, motivating him to stay focused on achieving his ultimate goal. They believed in his ability to overcome this setback, and their confidence in him became a source of inspiration. Paolo remained determined, viewing this obstacle as simply a part of his journey rather than its end.

Undeterred, Paolo decided to give his dream another shot. He spent a year training for his second attempt after his surgery, managing a demanding regimen while also adjusting to life as a college freshman.

With the support of his family and friends, Paolo set June 15, 2024, as the date for his run. However, in late May, Paolo's grandfather passed away. In his honor, Paolo dedicated the run to him. Meticulously planning every detail, Paolo and his team made sure everything was in place for his second attempt. He ran the first ten miles alone, setting the pace and focusing his mind on the journey ahead. At each rest stop, his team provided the necessary support by offering water, nutrition, and words of encouragement to keep his spirits high and determination strong.

Adding a deeply personal touch to his journey, Paolo carried a photo of his grandfather in his pouch throughout the entire one hundred-mile run. At the end of every ten-mile lap, he recorded and sent a video clip to his family in Italy. In each clip, he explained who was with him, what they meant to him, and shared a cherished memory of his grandfather.

Shortly after sunset on the day of the run, Paolo was more than halfway to achieving his goal. The atmosphere was filled with a mix of anticipation and excitement. Throughout the night, his friends and family continued to support him, taking shifts to stay awake and helping whenever needed.

Despite severe pain in his ankle, Paolo didn't quit. Instead, he adjusted his goal by mixing running with walking. By 9:15 a.m.

the following morning, after 28 hours, 13 minutes, and 46 seconds, Paolo completed one hundred consecutive miles. The moment was surreal, filled with cheers, tears, and an overwhelming sense of accomplishment.

It was an extraordinary achievement, a testament to his perseverance, mental fortitude, and the power of never giving up. When you don't succeed the first time, it's essential to trust the journey, give it another shot, involve others, and allow them to share in your success. Paolo's journey to one hundred miles is a reminder that with dedication, support, and belief, incredible goals can be achieved.

Life won't always go according to plan. No matter how clearly you set your objectives or how hard you work toward them, things won't always unfold the way you want. The best you can do is "control the controllables"—your attitude, effort, and the commitments you've made to yourself and others.

The fact that our fate is largely beyond our control is a difficult reality to accept. It's natural to feel anger and frustration when faced with unexpected challenges. Rather than denying these feelings, it's important to allow yourself to experience them. Then, look for the opportunities that these challenges may present. In his book, *The Obstacle is the Way*, author Ryan Holiday explains, "We can't change the obstacles themselves—that part of the equation is set—but the power of perspective can change how the obstacles appear."[36]

Andy Grove, former CEO of Intel, explains how different companies respond to significant obstacles: "Bad companies are destroyed by crises. Good companies survive them. Great companies are improved by them." This is true not just for organizations, but also for people. Life will inevitably throw unexpected challenges in your path, and while you may not always understand why things happen the way they do, how you respond to them is what matters.

It's perfectly normal to feel upset or frustrated when faced with obstacles, but it's important to acknowledge those feelings without letting them consume you. Even when the path ahead seems unclear, continue to move forward, trust the journey, and know that every experience, whether good or bad, shapes and strengthens you.

# Exercises

1) Identify Life's Curveballs.

List two unexpected changes or challenges life has thrown your way.

2) Analyze Your Reactions.

How did you resist or embrace each of these? What insights about yourself did you gain from them that can help you in your journey?

3) Let Go of Control.

What factors in your life do you try desperately to control but need to release?

# CHAPTER ELEVEN

# A MENSCH GOES FOR IT

You will miss 100% of the shots that you don't take.

Wayne Gretzky

In 2021, as the Senior Vice President for a medical technology company, I was responsible for several areas of the global business with seventy talented associates on my team. However, after more than eleven rewarding years, the job no longer fed my soul. Although I was helping improve patient lives, leading a large team, and traveling around the world, I felt a growing disconnect between the company's direction and who I strived to be as a leader. At the same time, Alex was in eleventh grade, preparing to visit colleges, and Marina was getting ready to begin her high school years. I wanted to participate more in their lives, especially since I hadn't experienced these moments with my father.

This realization about our careers and lives happens to many of us in our forties and fifties and is often dismissed as a "mid-life crisis." However, it's an important shift that shouldn't be ignored. As we age and grow, our experiences shape us, and what we want out of our lives also changes. Who we are in our twenties is not the same as who we are in our forties or fifties.

Many people misinterpret this shift as something negative, attributing it to dissatisfaction in personal relationships or their job. Ignoring this change can lead to less fulfillment, as we try to suppress the stress building inside of us. Remember, we have a choice in how we respond to these feelings. We can resist them or embrace them. Embracing them means leaning into who we are, which can be scary because who we are now is different from who we used to be. But this can be an exciting time, as we discover the person we have become.

In my case, embracing these feelings meant a significant career shift in my mid-forties. This decision was not made lightly. I spoke with my family, several friends, and mentors, giving their advice a lot of thought. The more I reflected on it, the clearer it became that I just had to go for it.

I left my role as a corporate executive to start a new career, leveraging my experience in building successful businesses and teams over the past twenty-five years. I recognized a widespread need for executives to receive guidance from someone with firsthand experience—someone who has "been there and done that." After researching and planning, I created a path that allowed me to make the change.

Transitioning into this new chapter was exciting and scary. I spent time reflecting on my journey, considering what I truly wanted to achieve. I set clear goals, which helped me focus my efforts and made the transition feel less overwhelming.

Connecting with my network was a key part of the process. I scheduled conversations with mentors and former colleagues, learning from their insights and experiences. Each discussion made me realize that many of them had faced similar challenges and successfully navigated their own transitions. Their stories inspired me and offered practical advice that I could apply to my situation.

As I moved forward, I volunteered with different organizations and mentored business leaders at various stages in their journeys. I helped them not only navigate their paths but also build their businesses and care for their teams. Sharing my experiences and offering guidance allowed me to find a renewed sense of purpose.

Every day brought new learning experiences, and I began to feel more comfortable. I was gaining confidence, and meeting so many great people along the way added so much to my experience. I also recognized that I was growing through this process. The fear that initially held me back started to fade as I embraced the opportunities that came my way.

With my family's full support, I did it. I took the necessary steps to continue my journey on a new path, and now I feel more fulfilled. Their belief in me helped me push through the uncertainties and stay focused on my goals. I'm excited to see where this new path will lead.

## Getting Unstuck

Following a family event in Pennsylvania in 2022, Mindy, Alex, Marina, and I spent a few days touring the area. During our visit, we met up with Mindy's long-time friend, Lauren. It had been twenty years since I had seen her, and when she asked how I was doing, I told her I was better than ever. I explained that I'd left my corporate job earlier that year because it no longer fed my soul and realized that it was time for a significant change.

Lauren then asked if I would speak with her husband, Chris. She shared that he had been in his retail career for about twenty years but wasn't happy anymore and didn't know what to do. I told her I would be happy to speak with him if he was interested.

I have always had a passion for helping people, especially those who want to take steps toward improving themselves and others. But I've learned that my support can only go so far. For someone to truly make a change in their life, they must be willing to put in the work to get to where they want to go.

From the beginning of my call with Chris, I could tell that he was committed and ready to move forward. His challenge was that he just didn't know where to start. We discussed tapping into his network to explore new career pathways and see which ones resonated most with him. He was already well on his way to doing this because he had taken the time to get on the phone with me.

At the end of the conversation, he said that he knew what he needed to do next. Several months later, he let me know how excited he was to start a new career in the insurance industry that would allow him to achieve his goals.

## You Are Not Your Job Title

Many people who feel stuck in their career paths never attempt to move forward because their identity is too closely tied to their job. After decades of climbing the ladder, they can't imagine being anything other than their professional title. The idea of making a career change, even if it's something they truly want to do, seems too overwhelming to consider.

Identifying yourself by your title is a dangerous trap. If you tie your identity too closely to what you do for a living, you risk losing sight of who you really are. This is where a personal identity statement can be powerful. When you clearly define your statement, including who you are and strive to be, it can serve as a "north star" to guide you through your journey.

Next time you're at a dinner party and feel tempted to ask a stranger, "What do you do for a living?" try something different. Instead, ask them what they like to do in their free time or to tell you about something they are passionate about. This simple shift in focus can help you—and others—see people for who they truly are, rather than just their job titles. Make it a habit to seek the whole person.

Detaching your value from your job title is challenging, especially in a society where your profession defines your social status. However, a generational shift is happening in our culture. Priorities are changing, and so is the way we think about work and choose to live our lives.

As career expert Bruce Feiler explains, "Today's workers rebuff the notion that each of us must follow a linear career—lock into a dream early, always climb higher, never stop until you reach the top. They resist having their lives summarized by a résumé... Many Americans still define career goals and try to achieve them, of course, but far more people experience an endless barrage of interruptions."[37]

These interruptions are the unexpected changes that can happen along our journey, whether positive or negative. This is why the question, "Where do you see yourself in ten years?" has become less relevant. The path to success is not linear; it is fluid and unique to everyone.

Feiler goes on to explain, "Today's workers are focused as much on the quality of their lives as on the quality of their jobs. Gallup found that millennials and members of Gen Z, who now make up half the workforce, place their greatest emphasis on well-being at work. Deloitte [a leading consulting firm] heard from the same group that work/life balance was their number one priority."

These "new rules for success" are changing the way we prioritize our work and live our lives. They push us to reconsider what truly matters. Learning that you are more than just your job title is key.

## Respectful Persistence

As you venture on a path to change and seek the support of others, be sure to practice respectful persistence. After working for a few months at my first professional job, my boss shared that the main reason he hired me over other candidates was because I had been "respectfully persistent" during the selection process. I followed up after each round of interviews, reiterating my qualifications and emphasizing my interest in the position. I also made sure to be firm and articulate enough to make a positive impression on the hiring teams, without coming across as too demanding.

Similarly, when Alex was pursuing a spot on a college baseball team, he sent numerous emails to coaches who had shown interest in him as a player. When his coach offered Alex a position on the team, he told Alex how much he appreciated his respectful persistence.

Pursuing your mission doesn't have to disrupt others or come across as overly intense. Find a way to strike a balance between being persistent and respectful. Doing so will not only serve you better throughout the process, but people will be more inclined to help along the way.

## Take Chances

When I decided to leave my corporate job and start my own business, it was a significant risk for me and my family. Despite having created a financial runway, walking away from a secure salary and corporate perks was daunting. Even if my new venture succeeded, it wouldn't be immediately profitable. However, I knew I had to take the leap. I didn't want fear of the unknown or the possibility of failure to hold me back. I had to follow my intuition, stay true to myself, make a commitment, and stick to it.

In his book, *The Obstacle is the Way*, Ryan Holiday notes, "So many people in our lives have preached the need to be realistic or conservative or worse—to not rock the boat. This is an enormous disadvantage when it comes to trying big things. Because though our doubts (and self-doubts) feel real, they have very little bearing on what is and isn't possible... Our perceptions determine, to an incredibly large degree, what we are and are not capable of."[38]

A great example of embracing this mindset is my friend and former coworker, Mael, who took several chances throughout his journey. Originally from France, I first met him at a global sales meeting in California. He immediately stood out to me with his engaged body language and the intelligent questions he asked during the session. At the time, Mael was working as a salesperson in France. Shortly after our meeting, he was offered an opportunity to temporarily relocate to Canada by one of our company leaders. After thinking about the offer, Mael and his family moved from Paris to Montreal.

Within a year, he became one of the top-performing sales representatives in our North American region. Initially, Mael was set to be in Canada for three years, but after his second year, an executive suggested he join my team in California for another two years. Recognizing his potential and interest in the opportunity, I welcomed him to my team once his visa to work in the United States was in place. Mael and his family relocated again, this time from Montreal to Southern California. He came up to speed quickly on our product lines and became a well-respected leader on the team.

As our company grew, I knew that Mael could make an even greater impact as a department leader. But he was set to go back to France in the next year, so it did not make sense for him to lead a team. I spoke with him about the situation and offered him the opportunity to stay in California long-term. He was thrilled and before long, he was an instrumental part of our leadership team.

Mael and his wife bought a house in San Diego County, where they still live today. Their daughter graduated from a local college, and his wife started a business selling French jewelry. Around this time, Mael started to feel a similar need for change brewing inside him, similar to what I had experienced a few years earlier.

Embracing it, he left his corporate position and now works with his wife at her jewelry business.

In a recent conversation with Mael about his journey over the past ten years, he reflected on his experiences. He shared that he never imagined living in the United States or running a jewelry business. He recognized the importance of trust—trust in the executive leader who first asked him to relocate, trust in me when he ventured into product marketing, and, most importantly, trust in himself to step outside his comfort zone and try something new.

When presented with unexpected opportunities, you might think, "I'm not an expert in that area" or "I don't know anyone." If you let these self-doubts dominate, you might miss an amazing opportunity. In Mael's case, he knew little about the North American market, product management, or the jewelry business but had the courage and work ethic to succeed. He took chances and ended up in a place far more fulfilling than he could have imagined.

## Take the Leap

If you feel a change stirring inside of you and can identify a mission that will drive you, then it's time to act. Don't wait for New Year's to make a resolution. If you know who you want to become, take a step forward to be that person now. As author James Clear points out, "Some people spend their entire lives waiting for the time to be right to make an improvement."[39] Don't wait. *Just do it.*

Taking action can look different for everyone. For me, it involved working towards several small changes in my life over a number of years. These gradual changes culminated when I transitioned to a new career path. Even a small step can get you started. It can be as simple as reconnecting with an old colleague or enrolling in an online course. Though these steps might seem insignificant, they can lead to meaningful change.

Some people hesitate to head down a new path because they feel like they don't have it entirely figured out. The truth is, life can't be fully planned, so there is no need to wait until you have all the details in place. All you need is an idea of where you want to head, then start moving in that direction. As the famous Chinese proverb says, "A journey of a thousand miles begins with a single step."

I also relate to what author Joanne Lipman describes as the "move before you move" concept. She explains, "Most people begin edging toward a major transformation, often unknowingly, before they embrace it wholeheartedly. For career changers, it may first emerge as a side hustle, a hobby, or even a seemingly random interest. They don't necessarily know where it's taking them. Nor do they necessarily have a goal in mind. 'Moving before you move' suggests, reassuringly, that we are laying the foundation—and are perhaps more prepared than we realize—for whatever comes next."[40]

The point is to just do something—any action that moves you forward. And once you start, don't stop. Meaningful, significant change can take time. Taking charge of your life is a process.

In my case, my new venture is just one step along my journey. There have been many steps before, and there will be more to come. Some will be difficult, and some will be rewarding. There is a pathway of steppingstones at my feet, and with each additional step I take, new stones appear as different options for progress along my path. I don't know exactly where they are heading, but I will do my best and enjoy the journey as I go.

Maybe not today, maybe not tomorrow, but at some point, you might find yourself at a crossroads, faced with a choice. It's at these moments that your willingness to embrace change and take action will define your path. Trust yourself, take that first step, and remember that each decision you make is part of your unique journey. I know you can do it.

# Exercises

1) Identify Desired Changes.

   As you reflect on your personal growth and the evolution of your life, consider what changes you'd like to make to your lifestyle or career. If you feel stuck, what mission or purpose can inspire and motivate you to move forward?

2) Recognize Obstacles.

   What obstacles or fears are currently preventing you from making the changes you identified in the previous step? Reflect on the specific challenges that are holding you back.

3) Implement Mensch Method Techniques.

   Considering the obstacles you identified, what mensch method techniques can you implement to help overcome these challenges and move towards your goals?

# CONCLUSION

Don't count the days, make the days count.

Muhammad Ali

In 1986, my mother was planning a trip to Italy with her boyfriend, Tony. Despite her excitement, she was anxious about leaving her three boys—aged 13, 10, and 8—behind. In a multipage letter to us, she wrote, "I can't not do things because I'm afraid." This letter turned out to be an essay of life lessons. Along with basic instructions on what to do while she was gone, it contained all the life advice she wanted to share with us. She wrote:

> "Carry your head high with the knowledge that you are doing the best you can and being the best kind of person you can be. But never forget the people who helped you along the way. Don't step on anyone else's toes to get where you want to be. Do everything legally and above-board. Respect other people and try to forgive them for the mistakes they make, even if they are at your expense. Find a way around it to come up on top... I have faith in the three of you, that you will turn out to be upstanding citizens, responsible adults, caring parents, loving and faithful husbands, friendly brothers, educated and bright students, hardworking employees or employers, sensitive

human beings, polite and respectful to all, etc. Whatever you do or become, be and do the best you can."

In other words, Mom was encouraging me and my brothers to be mensches. She highlighted key traits such as respecting others and doing our best—core principles of the mensch method.

Reflecting on these words, I realize how much they have shaped my life and guided my decisions. I learned what it meant to be a mensch at a very early age, when I faced an unimaginable tragedy that forced me to develop resilience and self-belief. Losing my father could have left me bitter and withdrawn, but instead, it instilled in me a determination to live a life of integrity, kindness, and strong character.

As I grew older, I recognized the impact that people and ideas could have on me, prompting me to choose my influences wisely. Progressing in my career, I came to understand the important role that others play in my life journey. I embraced this by cultivating my network, showing up for others, and allowing others to show up for me. It became clear that our journeys are intertwined, and the support we give and receive is crucial to our mutual growth and success.

Through my experience as a leader, I have learned the importance of demonstrating vulnerability and authenticity. These qualities, often seen as weaknesses in traditional leadership paradigms, are profound strengths. When I share my own struggles with others, it creates a space for them to do the same. This openness fosters trust and builds stronger, deeper relationships.

As I continue on my new career path, I focus on giving my best effort while maintaining my personal health and balance. I strive to honor the commitments I make to myself and others and have faith in my journey even when I'm not sure where it is taking me. I trust that the next step will become clear when it is supposed to. Most importantly, I remind myself that life is about being present in the moment and enjoying each step along the way.

So, how about you? What small, but impactful changes can you make to guide your journey towards the person and leader you aspire to be? Take an honest look at where you are today and identify the opportunities that can move you closer to your goals. Once you've done so, consider the small steps you can take to propel yourself forward. Change won't happen overnight, but when you have faith in your journey, put in the work, and live up to your standards, you will find fulfillment. Notice I use the word "fulfillment" instead of success. This is because everyone has their own definition of what success is. Living your life with a mensch mindset *will* lead to fulfillment.

Throughout my life, I've learned that being a mensch is not about grand gestures but about the small, consistent actions we take every day. It's about holding the door open for someone, offering a listening ear, or lending a helping hand. These seemingly small acts of kindness create a ripple effect, spreading positivity.

Most importantly, be sure to enjoy the journey. Neither your career path nor your life path will be a straight line. They will zig-zag and take unexpected twists and turns. Although these can be unnerving, embrace them with an open heart and a resilient spirit. Like you, I am still on my journey. After all, being a mensch is not an isolated event or a specific milestone to be met. It is a mindset met with action, and as long as you move forward each day by applying the concepts of *The Mensch Method*, you will have what you need to navigate your journey in a fulfilling way.

As you close this book and step back into your own life, remember that the journey of a thousand miles begins with a single step. Take that step with confidence, guided by the principles of *The Mensch Method*. Live fully, love deeply, and make a difference in the world. By doing so, you will not only find fulfillment but also inspire others to join you on this meaningful path. Together, we can create a ripple effect of positive change that will extend far beyond our own lives, impacting countless others and fostering a better world for generations to come.

# EPILOGUE

After sharing *The Mensch Method* with some of its earliest readers, I hosted an online roundtable to dive deeper into my journey and the concepts explored in the book. Here are some of their thoughtful questions and my responses.

**Roundtable Moderator:** To start us off, many of the early readers of your book are curious: What inspired you to write this book, and why did you choose mensch as the central theme?

**Todd Zive:** About two and a half years ago, a friend and I were talking about how much more divided the world felt compared to the past. There was this sense of disconnection—people ghosting each other, negativity dominating the media, and it felt like every word people said was being scrutinized. Common courtesy seemed to be fading away, with simple politeness, respect, and treating others with decency becoming less common. The world just felt darker.

During that conversation, my friend asked, "Have you ever thought about writing a book?" I laughed because the idea had never crossed my mind. I didn't think of myself as a writer. But he went on to say that my story had a way of uplifting people when I shared it in conversations. He believed that by writing a book, I could spread a message of positivity and hope to many more people who needed it. The idea of writing a book stuck with me, and after talking it over with my wife and a few close friends, I started thinking seriously about it. Everyone I spoke to was very supportive of the idea.

I didn't know where to begin, so I reached out to a few authors for advice, and they all said the same thing: "Just start writing every day." So, I did. As I wrote and shared my progress with others, the word mensch kept coming up. It's a word I've known my whole life and represents the characteristics that I strive to embody every day. Most people didn't know what it meant, but when I explained it to them, they loved it. Over time, I noticed that they started using mensch in their conversations, and that's when I knew it had to be the heart of the book. It also got me thinking that maybe this word could become part of everyday language and make a positive impact in the world.

**Moderator:** Some are also curious about your writing journey. What surprised you the most during the process of writing this book?

**Todd:** I was really surprised by how supportive people were and how deeply the mensch message resonated with them. Everyone who knew I was writing kept asking for updates, and their excitement fueled me to keep going, especially on the tougher days.

I was also struck by how many people said, "This is exactly what the world needs right now." It was eye-opening to see how much my story connected with others. What I didn't expect, though, was how challenging the writing process would be. Turning personal experiences into lessons that others could relate to was harder than I anticipated, but looking back, that challenge made the whole journey even more meaningful.

**Moderator:** You mentioned the challenges of writing about personal experiences. Was there a specific part of the book that was particularly difficult for you to write, and how did you get through it?

**Todd:** The hardest part was writing about my father's murder and the impact it had on me, which I cover in the first chapter. My mom had kept journals from my childhood, but I had avoided looking at them for years. To write this book honestly, I knew I had to go through them and confront those memories.

It wasn't easy, but it helped me better understand who I was then and how I've become the person I am today. Writing from the perspective of my younger self, not as an adult looking back, stirred up emotions I hadn't fully processed. As a child, I was just trying to navigate an incredibly complex and painful situation without the understanding I have now.

What got me through it, though, was facing those fears and drawing inspiration from other courageous authors. I asked my mom some difficult questions about my childhood and wrote down what I was feeling. Ultimately, working through those difficult parts helped me release pain I didn't even realize I was still carrying.

**Moderator:** You touched on your family in the book. Can you tell us a bit more about the paths your two brothers took?

**Todd:** I didn't go into much detail about their stories, as those are really theirs to tell. But I can say they've both built fulfilling lives. They are married, have wonderful kids, and are successful in their professions. Although we don't see each other as often as we'd like, since we live on opposite sides of the country, we stay connected through calls, FaceTime, and at family gatherings. Growing up with the loss of our dad shaped each of us differently, but we've all found our own way forward.

**Moderator:** For readers who feel inspired by the book but aren't sure where to start, what would you recommend they do next?

**Todd:** First, I'd applaud them for their dedication to improve. It shows they're serious about personal growth. My advice would be to start by taking just one small action today—one step toward becoming the person they want to be. Then take another small action tomorrow, and the day after that, and so on. I'd also remind them that growth is a journey, not a destination. Sometimes, the next step only becomes clear as you continue moving forward. It's important to be consistent and trust the process.

**Moderator:** And what would you say to someone who feels it might be too late for them to start living by the mensch method?

**Todd:** I'd say it's never too late for you. There's no deadline for becoming the best version of yourself. It doesn't matter where you are in life—the important thing is the choices you make from this point forward. You don't have to change everything all at once. It's about focusing on making one decision at a time that aligns with the mensch method, and those small steps will add up and lead to meaningful change.

**Moderator:** As *The Mensch Method* gains traction, how do you envision it spreading beyond the pages of this book?

**Todd:** I envision the mensch method becoming something that people not only talk about in their everyday lives—at home, at work, and in their communities—but also put into action. I'd be thrilled to see it improve the culture within organizations and help people live more fulfilling lives. Ultimately, if the mensch method can replace some of the negativity out there with positivity, I'm all for it.

**Moderator:** Given how quickly the world changes, how do you think the mensch method will hold up over time?

**Todd:** I'm confident the mensch method will stand the test of time because it's based on values that will always be relevant—character, integrity, kindness, and respect. The world will keep changing, and new challenges will arise, but those values will always matter. People will always respond to decency and authenticity, no matter what trends or technologies come along.

**Moderator:** What does the design on your book cover symbolize if anything?

**Todd:** The design on the cover represents the ripple effect—how even the smallest actions can create waves that spread and impact others. *The Mensch Method* is about living with integrity and kindness, which can inspire others and lead to positive change.

Just like when a pebble drops into a pond and creates ripples, every mensch-like act has the power to touch lives in ways we might never see.

**Moderator:** Finally, how can readers connect with you to learn more about *The Mensch Method* and apply it in their own lives?

**Todd:** The best way to connect with me is through my website, ToddZive.com, where anyone can learn more about how to apply *The Mensch Method* in their life and organization. I'm also active on LinkedIn so readers can reach me through that platform too.

# NOTES

## Introduction

1. Rosten, Leo. *The New Joys of Yiddish* New York: Three Rivers Press, 2001, s.v. "Mentsch," 232.
2. Rabbi Joshua Hammerman. "The Year of the Mensch," *New York Jewish Week*. March 26, 2019, https://www.jta.org/2019/03/26/ny/the-year-of-the-mensch.

## Chapter One

3. Neal Weinberg, "Druggist's Killer Sentenced to Life," *Springfield Sunday Republican*, May 30, 1981, excerpted in Fred Conrad, "Northwestern DA Sullivan Commemorates 30th Anniversary for Murder of Easthampton Pharmacist Leslie Zive," MassLive, May 27, 2011. https://www.masslive.com/news/2011/05/northwestern_da_office_recalls.html
4. "Ep. 11—Amy Purdy," interview by Jim Rome, May 20, 2021, in *The Reinvention Project*, produced by Cloud10, podcast, Spotify, 52:48, https://open.spotify.com/episode/6B7ZBl698fRyKk3v1b8syw
5. Amy Laskowski, "Travis Roy, 20 Years Later," *Bostonia*, Boston University, October 29, 2015, https://www.bu.edu/articles/2015/travis-roy-20-years-later/.

## Chapter Two

6. Achor, Shawn. *The Happiness Advantage: The Seven Principles of Positive Psychology that Fuel Success and Performance at Work.* Crown Currency, 2010.
7. *Encyclopaedia Britannica Online*, s.v., "San Francisco Earthquake of 1989," by Heather Campbell, last updated July 21, 2023, https://www.britannica.com/event/San-Francisco-earthquake-of-1989.
8. Alan Stein Jr. and Jon Sternfeld. *Raise Your Game* New York: Hachette Book Group, 2019, 27.

## Chapter Three

9. Hardy, Darren. *The Compound Effect.* Philadelphia, PA: Vanguard Press, 2010, 127.

10. Villalovos, Jaime. *Happy and Strong: Create Your Dream Life While Enjoying Your Journey.* Brentwood, TN: Forefront Books, 2022, 81.

11. Achor, Shawn. *Big Potential: How Transforming the Pursuit of Success Raises Our Achievement, Happiness, and Well-Being.* New York: Currency, 2018, 63.

12. Achor, Shawn. *Big Potential: How Transforming the Pursuit of Success Raises Our Achievement, Happiness, and Well-Being.* New York: Currency, 2018, 70.

13. "The Secret to a Happy Life w/ Dr. Robert Waldinger," March 21, 2023, in *The Ed Mylett Show*, produced by SXM Media, podcast, Spotify, https://open.spotify.com/episode/7nrKHeuMgqboKNmf6mOf-n0?si=13beb1047c834cbd

14. https://www.linkedin.com/posts/officialtonyrobbins_the-quality-of-our-life-is-the-quality-of-activity-7079459690438369281-xQqU/

## Chapter Four

15. Megan Sauer, "Mark Cuban Saw His Younger Self in This 'Shark Tank' Founder—And Offered Him a $1 Million Deal," Make It, CNBC, November 14, 2022, https://www.cnbc.com/2022/11/14/shark-tank-mark-cuban-saw-himself-in-collars-co-founder-justin-baer.html. The article references *Shark Tank*, season 14, episode 6, aired November 11, 2022, on ABC.

16. Alan Stein Jr. and Jon Sternfeld. *Raise Your Game.* New York: Hachette Book Group, 2019, 62.

17. Dweck, Carol S. *Mindset: The new psychology of success.* Random House, 2006.

## Chapter Five

18. Grant, Adam. *Give and Take: Why Helping Others Drives Our Success.* Orion, 2014.

19. Robert Waldinger, Marc Schulz, "The Lifelong Power of Close Relationships," *The Wall Street Journal*, January 13, 2023, https://www.wsj.com/articles/the-lifelong-power-of-close-relationships-11673625450

20. "The Secret to a Happy Life w/ Dr. Robert Waldinger," March 21, 2023, in *The Ed Mylett Show*, produced by SXM Media, podcast, Spotify, https://open.spotify.com/episode/7nrKHeuMgqboKNmf6mOfn0?si=13beb1047c834cbd

21. Sinek, Simon. *Leaders Eat Last: Why Some Teams Pull Together and Others Don't* 2014; repo. New York: Portfolio / Penguin, 2017, 21.

## Chapter Six

22. Diviney, Rich. *The Attributes: 25 Hidden Drivers of Optimal Performance.* Random House, 2021.

23. Bryant, Kobe. *The Mamba Mentality: How I Play.* MCD, 2018.

24. Magness, Steve. *Do Hard Things: Why We Get Resilience Wrong and the Surprising Science of Real Toughness.* HarperOne, 2022.

25. Selk, Jason. *Executive Toughness: The Mental-Training Program to Increase Your Leadership Performance.* McGraw Hill, 2011.

## Chapter Seven

26. Collins, Jim. *Good to Great: Why Some Companies Make the Leap... and Others Don't.* HarperCollins, 2001.

27. Clear, James. *Atomic Habits: An Easy & Proven Way to Build Good Habits & Break Bad Ones.* Random House Business Books, 2015.

28. Julian, Andre. *Streaking to Win: Using Micro-goals to Achieve the Success You Seek.* Andre Julian, 2021.

29. https://www.cnbc.com/amp/2023/11/17/the-no-1-regret-of-the-dying-i-see-it-all-the-time-says-psychologist-what-he-does-to-stop-it-now.html

30. "Ep. 37—James Lawrence," interview by Jim Rome, January 28, 2022, in *The Reinvention Project*, produced by Cloud10, podcast, Spotify, 32:45, https://open.spotify.com/episode/7qCCctwlaocX5AdXokNeqY?si=BN-0mdVA-QzSex-4ytGKM4w

31. Hay, Louise. *You Can Heal Your Life*. Hay House, 2004.

## Chapter Nine

32. Collins, Jim. *Good to Great: Why Some Companies Make the Leap... and Others Don't*. HarperCollins, 2001.

33. https://www.discprofile.com/what-is-disc

34. Brown, Brene. *The Power of Vulnerability*. Sounds True, 2012.

## Chapter Ten

35. Lipman, Joanne, "You're Already Moving Toward Your Next Career Small Steps on a New Path," *The Wall Street Journal*, March 11, 2023, https://www.wsj.com/articles/youre-already-moving-toward-your-next-career-a1d0cb42?mod=hp_listc_pos3 1/7

36. Holiday, Ryan. *The Obstacle is the Way: The Ancient Art of Turning Adversity into Advantage*. Generic, 2014.

## Chapter Eleven

37. Feiler, Bruce. "The New Rules of Success in a Post-Career World," *The Wall Street Journal*, June 2, 2023. Adapted from *The Search: Finding Meaningful Work in a Post-Career World,* Penguin Press, May 30, 2023.

38. Holiday, Ryan. *The Obstacle is the Way: The Ancient Art of Turning Adversity into Advantage*. Generic, 2014.

39. Clear, James. *Atomic Habits: An Easy & Proven Way to Build Good Habits & Break Bad Ones*. Random House Business Books, 2015.

40. Lipman, Joanne, "You're Already Moving Toward Your Next Career Small Steps on a New Path," *The Wall Street Journal*, March 11, 2023, https://www.wsj.com/articles/youre-already-moving-toward-your-next-career-a1d0cb42?mod=hp_listc_pos3 1/7

# ACKNOWLEDGMENTS

This book wouldn't have been possible without the incredible support of so many people. I'm truly grateful for everyone who played a part in this journey.

**Mindy Zive** – My wife and best friend. Mindy, you've been with me every step of the way, through the ups and downs, and I couldn't have done this without you. Your constant encouragement, careful edits, and endless patience helped me push through the toughest parts. Thank you for believing in me.

**Alex Zive** – My son, who spent countless hours helping me polish this manuscript. Alex, your sharp eye and honest feedback made all the difference. Your support gave me the confidence to keep going, and I'm so proud of the work we did together.

**Marina Zive** – My daughter, who always inspires me to be myself and share my story. Marina, your creative talents brought this book to life in ways I couldn't have imagined. Your ideas were a huge part of making this book what it is, and I'm so grateful for your help.

**Eydie Zive** – My mom, whose support and sacrifices have shaped so much of who I am today. Mom, you preserved the memories and documents that were crucial in writing the first chapter of this book. Your feedback and belief in me have been a constant source of encouragement, and I'm deeply grateful for everything you've done.

**Leslie Zive** – My father, whose life and untimely loss have shaped much of who I am today. Your memory is a constant source of strength and inspiration. This book, in many ways, is a tribute to the principles you lived by and instilled in me.

**Cynthia Allen** – My aunt, whose insightful questions and feedback were very helpful as I shaped this book. Aunt Cynthia, you introduced me to inspiring books that guided me along the way and spent countless hours helping with my early drafts. I'm deeply thankful for your support and guidance.

**Paul Samuels** – My uncle, who provided insight and feedback after reading through the first draft. Uncle Paul, your stories, some of which I was too young to remember, enriched the depth and context of my book. Your support throughout my life has meant so much to me, and I'm very grateful for you.

**David Moskowitz** – My cousin (on my mother's side), whose ideas and encouragement inspired me to add the epilogue and refine the manuscript one more time. David, your supportive comments kept me focused and motivated, and I greatly appreciate your thoughtful input.

**Monica Pierce, Whitney Bak, Liz Richards, and Jane Tabachnick –**
Thank you for your support at various stages of this journey. Your
help with outlining, editing, and the publishing process played a
key role in bringing this project to life. I appreciate each of your
contributions.

To all my family, friends, and professional network, I can't thank
you enough for your encouragement and support. Whether it was
offering a listening ear, sharing your thoughts, or simply cheering
me on, your support has been a cornerstone of this journey. I'm
incredibly fortunate to have such a wonderful group of people in
my life.

To the many authors, thinkers, and creators whose work inspired
and guided me along the way, thank you.

And finally, to my sweet goldendoodle, Olive, for your gentle
companionship. Your endless affection brought comfort and
motivation throughout the creation of this book.

Made in USA - Kendallville, IN
35472_9781959009207
12.21.2024 2016